Blessed is marriage

*A guide to the Beatitudes
for Catholic couples*

JOHN BOSIO

Blessed is
MARRIAGE

A **GUIDE** *to the* **BEATITUDES**
for **CATHOLIC COUPLES**

TWENTY
THIRD *23rd*
PUBLICATIONS
NEW LONDON, CT 06320
WWW.23RDPUBLICATIONS.COM

NIHIL OBSTAT
Richard H. Bulzacchelli, *Censor Deputatus*

IMPRIMATUR
✢ David R. Choby
Bishop of Nashville
January 24, 2012

THIRD PRINTING 2015

TWENTY-THIRD PUBLICATIONS
A Division of Bayard
One Montauk Avenue, Suite 200
New London, CT 06320
(860) 437-3012 or (800) 321-0411
www.23rdpublications.com

The Scripture passages contained herein are from the *New Revised Standard
Version of the Bible*, copyright ©1989, by the Division of Christian Education of
the National Council of Churches in the U.S.A. All rights reserved.

ISBN 978-1-58595-856-6
Printed in the U.S.A.

To my parents, Matteo and Maddalena,

to my wife, Teri,

to our children, Angela Bosio and
Laura and Robert Allen,

and to our grandson, Joseph David Allen.

Each taught me in their unique way how to love.

CONTENTS

FOREWORD

With the plethora of "how-to" books on the market today, it is refreshing to find one with solid theological and pastoral principles directed to married couples. I thoroughly enjoyed *Blessed Is Marriage: A Guide to the Beatitudes for Catholic Couples*. The author, John Bosio, draws from his experience as a family therapist and committed believer to provide a path for a loving marriage. In this engaging book, the reader will encounter true-to-life resurrection stories, often beginning with the death that brings a couple to a therapist. Timely quotes from the recent U.S. bishops' pastoral *Marriage: Love and Life in the Divine Plan* as well as links to Pope Benedict XVI's *Jesus of Nazareth* provide both theological grounding and inspiration about married life.

Readers seek to be inspired as well as informed, and this book speaks to both head and heart. With vignettes drawn from actual couples who seek help in therapy, the book proclaims the importance of the promises made and kept in marriage and the vital nature of marriage-friendly therapy as it encourages couples that the desire to seek help is a sign of health. A quote from Thornton Wilder's *The Skin of Our Teeth* truly summarizes this walk through the Beatitudes: "I married you because you gave me a promise. That promise made up for your faults. And the promise I gave you made up for mine. Two imperfect people got married, and it was the promise that made the marriage." I would add that the power to live that promise is a grace beyond the couple...the power of God in whom they trust guiding them through the joys and sorrows of every marriage.

Most Reverend Joseph E. Kurtz, DD
Archbishop of Louisville

ACKNOWLEDGMENTS

One of the themes interwoven in the pages of *Blessed Is Marriage: A Guide to the Beatitudes for Catholic Couples* is the idea that we learn from one another. As individuals and as married couples, our lives and love stories are connected and influence one another. This book is the fruit of many people, from the many authors who have inspired me to write, to my extended family, to our friends and colleagues, to the people I met around the world in my travels, and to the couples I worked with in counseling. In these chapters the names of couples described in counseling situations have been changed to protect their confidentiality.

Here I want to personally acknowledge and recognize some of the individuals who took time to read my manuscript and gave me their feedback and guidance. My appreciation goes to: Most Reverend Joseph E. Kurtz, DD, archbishop of Louisville; Most Reverend David R. Choby, bishop of Nashville; Richard H. Bulzacchelli, STL, associate professor of theology at Aquinas College, Nashville, Tennessee; Christine Codden, director of the Office of Marriage and Family for the Diocese of Saint Cloud, Minnesota, and past president of the National Association of Catholic Family Ministers; Valerie and Mike Conzett, Family Life Office, Archdiocese of Omaha; Lorrie and Don Gramer, Family Life directors, Diocese of Rockford, and Lorrie is president of the National Association of Family Life Ministers; Mr. Frank Hannigan, director, Family Ministries Office, Archdiocese of Chicago; Matthew Kelly, founder of The Dynamic Catholic Institute; Judith Leonard, director, Family Life and Natural Family Planning, Diocese of Wichita; Dr. H. Richard McCord, past executive director, Secretariat of Laity, Marriage, Family Life, and Youth; Msgr. Thomas Tank, pastor, Church of the Ascension, Overland Park, Kansas; Dr. Denny and Karen Schemmel, family therapist and my mentor, Overland Park, Kansas; and Mr. Steve Zanolini.

Special thanks to Teri, my wife, who has been my most honest critic and valuable advisor.

God's love song

Deep within your heart,
if you listen,
you hear God's voice.[1]

He sings to you his eternal love song:
the song through which he created the universe,
the stars and the moon, the flowers,
*   the birds and all creatures.*

It is the song through which God
formed you in your mother's womb

---

1. Pope Benedict XVI, *Greeting to the Youth of London after Mass in Westminster Cathedral*, September 18, 2010 (www.thepapalvisit.org.uk/Replay-the-Visit/Speeches/Speeches-18-September/Pope-Benedict-s-Message-to-Young-People).

"Deep within your heart, he is calling you to spend time with him in prayer....We need to make space for silence, because it is in silence that we find God, and in silence that we discover our true self. And in discovering our true self, we discover the particular vocation which God has given us for the building up of his Church and the redemption of our world."

and called you out of it
to love him and to serve him.

God's song is the music that attracted you to your spouse;
the rhythm that moves you to dance together;
the melody that leads you to grow in love with each other;
and the voice that calls you to serve God
as a married couple.

God created man and woman and fashioned them in his own image. He invited them to join him in singing his eternal love song. Unfortunately, Adam and Eve chose to sing their own song. Their disobedience broke their relationship with God and disrupted the harmony that existed between man and woman.[2]

In his immense love for us, the Father sent his Son to restore our relationship with himself. Jesus came and gave himself so totally to us that he died on the cross. Through his death and Resurrection, he redeemed us. He became our advocate and our guide.

On your wedding day you chose marriage as your vocation and as your path to holiness. You joined hands with your spouse, and together you embraced Christ as your partner on your journey to God.

As a couple you are a duo trying to sing God's song and to dance to its rhythm. Saint Augustine exhorts us, "Sing with your voices, your hearts, your lips and your lives; sing to the Lord a new song."[3] In sing-

---

2. *Catechism of the Catholic Church*, #400.

"The harmony in which they had found themselves, thanks to original justice, is now destroyed: the control of the soul's spiritual faculties over the body is shattered; the union of man and woman becomes subject to tension, their relations henceforth marked by lust and domination."

3. Saint Augustine, *Sermon* 34.1–3, 5–6; CCl 41, 424–426. Found April 9, 2011 at www.vatican.va/spirit/documents/spirit_20010508_agostino-vescovo_en.html.

ing God's love song, there are times when you and your spouse make wonderful harmony together, and there are also times when you are out of tune, forget the lyrics, or don't feel like singing.

All of us have a lot to learn about singing God's love song. God is love. He alone can teach us and help us with his grace.[4] All we need to do is ask, as Jesus told us: "I will do whatever you ask in my name, so that the Father may be glorified in the Son" (John 14:13).

Let Mary and Joseph be your models of a married couple's faithful obedience to God. Ask for their intercession to help you grow in faith. The greater your faith, the clearer you hear God's voice, and the happier you will be in your marriage.

I hope that through your reading this book you will become better attuned to the sound of God's voice and will follow it.

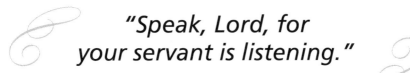

"Speak, Lord, for your servant is listening."

1 SAMUEL 3:9

In the chapters of this book, we will explore the Beatitudes as the loving attitudes for our Christian life. These attitudes turn us toward God. They open our hearts to hear his voice. Pope Benedict XVI told the Catholic youth gathered in London on September 18, 2010, "I ask

---

4. Pope Benedict XVI, *Greeting to the Youth of London after Mass in Westminster Cathedral*, September 18, 2010 (www.zenit.org/article-30401?l=english).

"Every day we have to choose to love, and this requires help, the help that comes from Christ, from prayer and from the wisdom found in his word, and from the grace which he bestows on us in the sacraments of his Church."

you to look into your heart each day to find the source of all true love. Jesus is always there, quietly waiting for us to be still with him and to hear his voice." This book is written in the spirit of the pope's invitation. Read these pages and listen to God's voice. With Jesus' help, learn to sing God's love song and to dance to its rhythm. You will find joy in your life and in your marriage.

■ Where do I start?

You may be reading this book to find inspiration and guidance for growth in your marriage. If that is the case, you have a wonderful goal. I believe that you will find what you are looking for in the pages that follow. My premise is that to grow in love and to find happiness in the company of our spouse, we need to grow in holiness. Holiness attunes our hearts to God's song and prepares us to love. However, growth in holiness and love will not happen by simply reading a book. They require a change of attitude. This book will guide you to align your own attitudes with Jesus' good counsel.

In each chapter, you will find a section titled "Where Do I Start?" Listed there are practical steps you can take each day to grow in holiness and to strengthen your bond with your spouse. Do what is suggested, regardless of whether your spouse does the same. Do it out of love. You may be surprised to find that your spouse will respond in kind because "love grows through love."[5]

After each chapter, you will also find two sets of questions. One is provided as a guide for your private conversation with your spouse. The other is better suited for sharing among couples in a group. This book is an excellent resource for couples who meet in small groups to

---

5. Pope Benedict XVI, *Deus Caritas Est* (Vatican City: December 25, 2005), Paragraph 18.

support one another, pray together, and help each other grow in their marriages.

Reading this book can become your own private retreat at home. To benefit the most from it, read a chapter a week. In between readings, reflect on the content of the chapter, practice the acts of love suggested, and pray for your spouse. Remember, growth is gradual and comes about through change, and change begins with you. Change begins with me. Let the words of the hymn "Let there be Peace on Earth," which proclaims that peace begins with each of us, be a reminder to you that your journey to a greater love for God and for your spouse begins with you today.

CHAPTER ONE

Blessed are they...

What happened to us?

Married two years and parents of a very active one-year-old, Jim and Rose are tired, stressed out, and angry at each other. They are both working full time, and each has career aspirations. This evening Rose is in the living room folding the laundry and playing with their son, Charlie. Jim is in the garage working on his favorite hobby, his car. Rose wonders in silence, *What has happened to us? The wedding pictures are still on the coffee table and yet, how I feel today and how I felt in the early days of our marriage are like day and night. How did we end up feeling so distant?*

Marriage is like riding a canoe

Dr. William Doherty, PhD, author of the book *Take Back Your Marriage*,[6] writes that getting married is like launching a trip on the Mississippi river with a canoe. You set out in Saint Paul, Minnesota,

---

6. William Doherty, *Take Back Your Marriage* (New York: Guilford Press, 2001), p. 11.

and unless you paddle fast and together, the current takes you south to places you did not intend to visit.

After the wedding, if you rely solely on your instincts and feelings to keep your relationship going, your canoe drifts, pulled by the currents of daily activities. Unless you paddle together, you slowly and unintentionally drift apart. At the start of your journey, you find the novelty of married life enjoyable. Then, gradually, you begin to take each other for granted. Each wants to go in a different direction, do different things. When children are born, tending to their needs seems to take over your life. Conflicts arise that are not resolved. Negative feelings of frustration and anger are left to fester. The good feelings you had for each other slowly evaporate, your relationship gradually weakens, and, after so much drifting, one or both of you think about jumping ship. Unfortunately, this is the path taken by many couples. Recent research indicates that for many couples the bliss fades after three years, and the advent of children increases the tension and the stress in the family. Most divorces take place during the first seven years.

Our attitudes make a difference

Finding happiness on the marriage voyage requires learning to paddle together and moving forward in the same direction. However, most spouses find it difficult to agree on a common direction, much less to paddle as a team.

Paddling in synchrony requires a unique mind-set, a special attitude. Winston Churchill is quoted to have said, "Attitude is a little thing that makes a big difference." Our attitudes represent our stance in life, what we believe about ourselves and about others. Our attitudes are manifested in the values we embrace, in how we think, in what we say, and, ultimately, in what we do. As such, our attitudes greatly affect the quality of the marital relationship and the willingness of partners to coordinate their efforts. Successful couples develop attitudes that allow them to agree on a common direction for their life. They embrace a set of values that act as a compass on their journey. Their attitudes encourage them to put aside their individual self-interests in order to collaborate, to paddle together for the sake of the relationship.

The guidance from our Christian faith

Christian husbands and wives learn through the practice of their faith both the direction for their marriage voyage and the collaborative spirit needed to stay on course. They learn from the Christian tradition that their life together has a special meaning. It is a vocation. For them marriage is not a private affair between two people caught up in romantic infatuation. Christian spouses believe that their commitment to each other is a response to God's call to love him and to be a sacrament of his love to one another, to their family, and to their community. Their relationship is a journey toward God and toward each other that leads them to holiness and to happiness.

When you entered Christian marriage, you embraced Christ as your partner, teacher, and guide on your journey. He sits with you in your canoe, ready to help. In the chapters of this book, you will learn from Jesus the direction for your voyage and the loving attitudes that make it possible for you and your spouse to paddle together and make progress toward your destination.

The benefit of practicing our faith

Psychologists and marriage therapists write articles and books about the behaviors and skills that help couples grow in their relationship. However, in spite of all the good advice from the social sciences, couples continue to struggle and break up, and the divorce rate is still too high. Fortunately, couples of faith have at their disposal not only the behaviors and skills recommended by marriage experts but also the guidance of the Holy Spirit and the power of God's grace.

Researchers are finding that spouses who pray and practice their religion are less likely to get sidetracked on their voyage and to divorce. Kenneth Pargamen and Annette Mahoney,[7] professors of psychology at Bowling Green State University, are finding in their research that spouses that go to church regularly have a higher degree of marital satisfaction and commitment, as well as better communication and conflict resolution skills.

It may be that faith-practicing couples are more successful in their marriage because of the Christian attitudes they learn from Christ, which Paul summarizes for the Colossians: "Clothe yourselves with compassion, kindness, humility, meekness, and patience. Bear with one another and…forgive each other" (3:12–13). These are Christ's attitudes, which he proclaimed in the Sermon on the Mount. As Peter exhorts us, "Arm yourselves also with the same intention [as Christ]… so as to live…by the will of God" (1 Peter 4:1–2).

The loving attitudes

John Paul II told the youth gathered in Toronto for the Seventeenth World Youth Day on July 25, 2002, that God created man and woman to be happy together, and the Sermon on the Mount is the map for our journey to such happiness.[8]

---

7. David Yonke, "Happy Marriage Begins at Church Door BGSU Study Reports," *Toledo Blade*, April 14, 2007.

8. John Paul II, *Papal Welcoming Ceremony, Seventeenth World Youth Day*, Toronto, July 25, 2002 (www.vatican.va/holy_father/john_paul_ii/speeches/2002/july/documents/hf_jp-ii_spe_20020725_wyd-address-youth_en.html).

> "It is told in the Book of Genesis: God created man and woman in a paradise, Eden, because he wanted them to be happy.…The 'Sermon on the Mount' marks out the map of this journey. The eight Beatitudes are the road signs that show the way."

At the start of his ministry, Jesus walked up a hill, and after he sat down, he began to teach his disciples and the crowd that had gathered by proclaiming:

> *Blessed are the poor in spirit,*
> *for theirs is the kingdom of heaven.*
> *Blessed are those who mourn,*
> *for they will be comforted.*
> *Blessed are the meek,*
> *for they will inherit the earth.*
> *Blessed are those who hunger and thirst for righteousness,*
> *for they will be filled.*
> *Blessed are the merciful,*
> *for they will receive mercy.*
> *Blessed are the pure in heart,*
> *for they will see God.*
> *Blessed are the peacemakers,*
> *for they will be called children of God.*
> *Blessed are those who are persecuted for righteousness' sake,*
> *for theirs is the kingdom of heaven.*

■ MATTHEW 5:3–10

Poverty in spirit, mourning, meekness, mercifulness, purity in heart, peacefulness, and righteousness are the loving attitudes that open our heart to God and to one another. They help us paddle together in our marriage. They help us find the joy that Jesus promised: "I have said these things to you so that my joy may be in you, and that your joy may be complete" (John 15:11).

Happiness flows from holiness

Jesus gave us the Beatitudes, our loving attitudes,[9] as the path to holiness. It is holiness that brings happiness. Holiness brings joy and contentment. As Saint Paul writes, "…for I have learned to be content with whatever I have" (Philippians 4:11). Benedict XVI reminds us that holiness is within reach to all of us. He writes, "Holiness does not consist in never having erred or sinned. Holiness," he adds, "increases the capacity for conversion, for repentance, for willingness to start again and, especially, for reconciliation and forgiveness."[10]

The marriage voyage is challenging and demanding. But Christ is present with us and through his grace helps us make progress on our journey in spite of our weaknesses and sinfulness.

The power of grace

Although researchers are finding that spouses who pray and practice their faith are more likely to stay together and have a higher degree of marital satisfaction, the daily life of the Christian couple is not easier than anyone else's. Misunderstandings, conflicts, disappointments, and other difficulties are inevitable in a couple's life.

---

9. John Paul II, *The Splendor of Truth* (Vatican City: August 6, 1993), #16.

> "The Beatitudes are not specifically concerned with certain particular rules of behavior. Rather, they speak of basic attitudes and dispositions in life."

Also: John Paul II, *Homily at the Mount of the Beatitudes*, March 2000 (www.vatican.va/holy_father/john_paul_ii/travels/documents/hf_jp-ii_hom_20000324_korazim-israel_en.html).

> "Sinai and the Mount of the Beatitudes offer us the roadmap of our Christian life and a summary of our responsibilities to God and neighbor."

10. Benedict XVI, *General Audience*, January 31, 2007 (www.vatican.va/holy_father/benedict_xvi/audiences/2007/documents/hf_ben-xvi_aud_20070131_en.html).

What helps Christian spouses to cope with their daily challenges and to overcome their human limitations and sinfulness is the effect of God's grace.

Blessed Pope John Paul II told us, "Jesus does not stand by and leave you alone to face the challenge. He is always with you to transform your weakness into strength. Trust him when he says: 'My grace is enough for you, for my power is made perfect in weakness' (2 Corinthians 12:9)!"[11] When we put our trust in Christ's power and follow him, we grow in holiness and find happiness.

■ Where do I start?

In each chapter of this book, you will be asked to make a small change in your life that will take you closer to your goal of a more loving marriage. Consider the suggestions below, and do as many as you can.

- Commit to reading the chapters of this book.

- Commit five minutes each day to silently listen to God's voice. Identify a time and place where you can do so.

- Say a prayer of thanksgiving to God for the gift that your spouse is to you.

- Ask yourself, "Are we drifting?" Reflect on this for a few minutes.

- Do something small that you know your spouse will appreciate.

---

11. John Paul II, *Homily at the Mount of the Beatitudes*, March 2000.

Jim and Rose and you

To stop their drifting, Jim and Rose needed to acknowledge that they were going in the wrong direction and turn to each other and to God for help. When you acknowledge your personal failings and turn to God and to each other for help, you are ready to hear God's voice and to receive his graces. God's grace gives you the courage to reset the course of your journey and to choose the direction that leads to him. It is through God's grace that you and your spouse help one another toward holiness; as the *Catechism of the Catholic Church* teaches us, "By this grace they 'help one another to attain holiness.'"[12] God's grace and the spouses' openness to receive it are some of the reasons faith-practicing couples have a higher degree of marital satisfaction.

In the coming chapters, we will explore the loving attitudes for a happy marriage. These are drawn from Jesus' Beatitudes which, according to the *Catechism*, "shed light on the actions and attitudes characteristic of the Christian life."[13] We will ask: What does it mean for husband and wife to be poor in spirit, to be meek, and to mourn? We will explore how spouses hunger for righteousness, are merciful, have a clean heart, and become peacemakers, as Jesus commands. Finally, we will reflect on the threats to marriage present in our age and on what spouses are to do to inherit the kingdom.

---

12. *Catechism of the Catholic Church*, #1641.

13. *Catechism of the Catholic Church*, #1717.

■ Prayer

O come, let us sing to the Lord;
  let us make a joyful noise to the rock of our salvation!
Let us come into his presence with thanksgiving;
  let us make a joyful noise to him with songs of praise!
For the Lord is a great God,
  and a great King above all gods.
In his hand are the depths of the earth;
  the heights of the mountains are his also.
The sea is his, for he made it,
  and the dry land, which his hands have formed.

O come, let us worship and bow down,
  let us kneel before the Lord, our Maker!
For he is our God,
  and we are the people of his pasture,
  and the sheep of his hand.

O that today you would listen to his voice!
  Do not harden your hearts...

■ PSALM 95:1–8

■ QUESTIONS FOR **A COUPLE'S PRIVATE REFLECTION**

- Is our marriage canoe moving in the right direction?

- Are we drifting?

- How good are we at paddling together?

- What causes us to get out of sync?

- What are our common dreams as a couple?

- How do we experience the effect of God's grace in our marriage?

■ QUESTIONS FOR **GROUP SHARING**

- What stood out for me or struck me in reading this chapter?

- In what situations do I feel that our life together is like an adventure in a canoe?

- How does my Christian faith encourage me to collaborate with my spouse?

- If God were to use a contemporary song to express his love for me, what song would he pick, and why?

- How often do I turn to God for help to resolve conflicts in our relationship?

- Can you think of a couple who models the loving attitudes expressed in the Beatitudes in their marriage?

CHAPTER TWO

Stay turned toward God and each other

Blessed are the poor in spirit…

Remember your first kiss

The young couple sitting in my office made an appointment to talk about their relationship because, as Mary informed me on the phone, "We seem to be arguing all the time." They had been married three years.

After listening to their litany of daily skirmishes over money, house chores, sex, in-laws, and conflicts of schedules, I asked them to put aside all their hurt and angry feelings, to close their eyes, and to recall a good moment in their relationship. To guide them on this task, I asked, "Do you remember the first time you kissed? How did you feel?"

After a long silence, Joe opened his eyes and reached out to grab Mary's hand. They looked at each other and they smiled. I said, "From your looks and gestures I gather there is a story here. Can you share it with me?"

Mary said bashfully, "Joe and I were very good friends for over a year before we started dating. I'm not sure why, but we dated for several months before we ever kissed. I still remember that first kiss very vividly." She looked at Joe and smiled. He nodded in agreement. "One evening, after a date, we were sitting in Joe's car in the driveway of my parents' home. We were talking and listening to music. At one point Joe turned to me and slowly, almost hesitantly, kissed me and whispered, 'I love you.' My mind was flooded with emotions. I knew at that moment that our relationship had changed, and I was scared. Words came out of my mouth, 'I love you too.' I felt that this kiss was a turning point in my life. I explained to Joe, 'I am very happy, but I am also a little scared.' He smiled, then he said, 'I understand. I feel the same way.' After a few moments of silence he added, 'Do you want to pray?' No guy had ever suggested prayer on a date. But prayer at that moment was also what I wanted. I needed God's help. So we said the Our Father together."

In the retelling and reliving of that wonderful moment, Joe and Mary reconnected again and were able to look at their drifting relationship in a new way. They were reminded of the good qualities that attracted them to each other. They were also reminded of their need for God in times like this, and of the power of prayer.

Blessed are the poor in spirit

In the Gospel of Matthew, Jesus reveals the roadmap to the joy of the kingdom in the eight Beatitudes. The first among these proclaims, "Blessed are the poor in spirit, for theirs is the kingdom of heaven" (Matthew 5:3). With this statement, Jesus exhorts us to take our first step toward holiness. Taking this first step means turning ourselves toward God, like a flower in the field turns toward the sun to receive life. A Franciscan proverb describes poverty in spirit with these words: "The joy of poverty is not to have nothing in this world; the joy of poverty is to have nothing but God."

Jim Forest, author of *The Ladder of the Beatitudes*, writes, "Poverty of spirit is my awareness that I need God's help and mercy more than I need anything else."[14] Such total deference to God is the essence of this Beatitude and is achieved only with the help of the Holy Spirit. At baptism and later at confirmation, Christians receive the spiritual gift of "Fear of the Lord," the gift of awe and reverence for God. Through this gift the Holy Spirit helps Christians grow in humility and respect toward God and one another.

When, in reverence, we turn ourselves toward God and we listen to his voice, we find direction for our marriage. He is telling us to turn toward each other and to love one another as he loves us (John 13:34). Spousal love requires the acknowledgement of our own poverty—our dependence and need for one another. Loving spouses turn away from everything else and turn toward one another. Turning toward God and toward each other is an expression of poverty in spirit.

Stay turned toward each other

John Gottman, professor of psychology at the University of Washington, writes that a couple's commitment to staying "turned toward each other"[15] is one of the keys to marital success. In his research he found that when spouses make a choice to stay turned toward each other, they "remain emotionally engaged and stay married."[16] Spouses that

---

14. Jim Forest, *The Ladder of the Beatitudes* (New York: Orbis Books, 1999), p. 22.

15. John M. Gottman, PhD, and Nan Silver, *The Seven Principles for Making Marriage Work* (New York: Crown Publishers, Inc., 1999), p. 80.

16. *Ibid.,* p. 80.

are turned toward each other think about one another in everything they do; they keep in mind what the other likes and dislikes. They do little things for the pleasure of the other. They show interest in what the other is doing. They are aware of each other's needs. They appreciate each other and they do not take each other for granted. Turning toward each other in these ways, writes Gottman, "is the basis of emotional connection, romance, passion, and a good sex life."[17] Staying turned toward each other honors the promises you made on your wedding day.

Michele Weiner-Davis, a marriage and family therapist and a renowned author, states in an article posted on the Forever Families website that the main cause of today's breakdown in marriages is that of misplaced priorities. "People spend time on their careers, their kids, community affairs, hobbies, sports."[18] When this happens, marriage, unfortunately, takes a back seat. This misplacement of priorities causes spouses to move in different directions and at different paces. They gradually turn away from each other, and discontentment enters into their marriage.

The attitude of poverty in spirit helps us stay turned toward God and toward our spouse. It helps us stay connected and able to hear God's voice and the voice of our spouse.

■ Where do I start?

Start with the most fundamental of your daily interactions: the act of listening. Consider the following suggestions and do as many as you can.

---

17. *Ibid.*, p. 80.

18. Megan Northrup, *Forever Families—Immunized Against Infidelity: "Affair-proofing" Your Marriage* (http://foreverfamilies.byu.edu/Article.aspx?a=47), December 1, 2011.

- Listen to your spouse without interrupting.

- Give your full attention to hear what your spouse is saying.

- Avoid jumping to conclusions on what your spouse might mean.

- Give your spouse the benefit of the doubt.

- If you are not sure you understand, respectfully ask your spouse to explain.

- Consider your spouse's ideas, suggestions, and advice with an open mind.

- If you want to improve your listening skills, consider reading the book *Talking and Listening Together: Couple Communication One*, by Sherod Miller and Minnesota Family Study Center.

Effective listening, whether to God or to our spouse, requires poverty in spirit. It requires that we acknowledge our need to hear what our spouse is thinking, feeling, or wanting. We are in a relationship, and the richness of our marriage depends on our ability to stay connected, to understand our spouse, and to move in sync with each other. Without listening to each other, spouses cannot paddle together, and they slowly drift apart.

Prayer—An admission of our poverty

In their first kiss Mary and Joe came face-to-face with the mystery of their relationship and their own limitations. Feeling overwhelmed with joy and at the same time scared, they reached out beyond themselves to God for help.

Like Mary and Joe, all spouses feel overwhelmed and scared from time to time. Events like illnesses, financial setbacks, job losses, deaths in the family, geographic relocations, and others make spouses realize how poor in spirit they are and how much they need others and God.

When we pray, we acknowledge God's goodness and power, as well as our human limitations and our need for his graces. Prayer is both a sign of poverty in spirit and a means to grow in it.

Family ritual

Years later I saw Joe and Mary at a gathering. They had two beautiful girls with them. I asked if they remembered our first meeting in my office. They smiled. Then Joe said in reference to the story of their first kiss, "That first kiss marked not only the start of our relationship but also the beginning of a family tradition. Throughout our marriage, whenever one of us is scared or concerned about something or wants to celebrate a special event, we approach the other with the question 'Do you want to pray?' This usually happens late in the evening, when we are in bed, just before we fall asleep. There have been times when we have invited the girls to join us. And so, we all crowd on our bed for an intimate moment of prayer, and together we say the Our Father."

■ Prayer

Protect me, O God, for in you I take refuge.
I say to the Lord, "You are my Lord;
*   I have no good apart from you."*

I bless the Lord who gives me counsel;
*   in the night also my heart instructs me.*
I keep the Lord always before me;
*   because he is at my right hand, I shall not be moved.*

Therefore my heart is glad, and my soul rejoices;
*   my body also rests secure.*

You show me the path of life.
*   In your presence there is fullness of joy;*
*   in your right hand are pleasures forevermore.*

■ PSALM 16:1–2, 7–9, 11

■ QUESTIONS FOR **A COUPLE'S PRIVATE REFLECTION**

- Do you remember the first time you kissed your spouse? How did you feel?

- What does your spouse do that tells you that he or she is turned toward you?

- How easy is it for you to turn to God and to your spouse for help?

- Do you pray together?

- List situations in which you are reminded that you are in need of God's help.

■ QUESTIONS FOR **GROUP SHARING**

- What did your parents teach you about prayer? How did they pray?

- Did you pray together when you were engaged, as Joe and Mary did? How do you pray today?

- Do you agree that praying is an admission of poverty?

- Does the concept of "staying turned toward each other" make sense to you?

- In your day-to-day interactions what do you do to stay turned toward your spouse?

- Can you think of a couple who models the loving attitude of poverty in spirit in their marriage?

"Blessed are the poor in spirit, for theirs is the kingdom of heaven."

CHAPTER THREE

Accept what is

Blessed are those who mourn…

I don't know what to do

One evening, during one of my business trips, I was having dinner with Jack, a colleague, at the restaurant in our hotel. At one point toward the end of the meal, he said, "I don't know what to do." He paused to get my full attention. "My manager tells me that to make progress in my career I need to be willing to relocate. He says that mobility is very important for my advancement with the company. Unfortunately, Grace, my wife, does not want to move to another city. She was born in our town and all of her family lives near us. She has made it very clear to me that she is not moving." Jack stopped to sip his wine, and then he continued with a defiant smirk on his face, "I'm so angry with Grace that a few weeks ago I thought of applying for a job-opening in Boston, just to see what she would do." He stopped. We sat in silence for a long time. Then, with a determined look, he took a deep breath and, shaking his head, said, "I don't want to put my career before Grace's wishes, but I also don't want to have limited opportunities for advancement because of her unwillingness to move. Do you understand my situation? What do you think?"

Our conversation went on for some time, revealing that the conflict over relocating was just one of many for this couple. At the end of the evening, Jack commented, "This subject makes me very depressed. You know that I would never leave Grace! I am committed to her and to my children. We will be married ten years in a few months. I just needed to vent. Thanks for listening."

Mourning our losses

My friend was mourning the loss of his dreams. He had imagined a blissful marriage without conflicts, and a glamorous career without obstacles. He expected to be moving up and growing with the company. The reality of life was hitting him hard, and he was striving to accept it.

Grieving our losses, whether physical, emotional, or spiritual, is part of the human condition. The mourning process is an essential step in healing and growing. It allows us to face reality, to recognize and accept our limitations and losses, and to make the changes that are necessary to cope and to adjust to what is ahead.

Pope Benedict XVI writes that mourning helps because it teaches us "to hope and to love again."[19] In proclaiming, "Blessed are those who mourn" (Matthew 5:4), Jesus is inviting us to let our pains remind us of our humanness, to embrace our sorrows as a means to holiness, and to turn to God for help and consolation as we look to the future with hope.

---

19. Joseph Ratzinger, *Jesus of Nazareth* (New York: Doubleday, 2007), p. 86.

Inevitable pain and sacrifice

Marriage is not immune from the experience of loss and suffering. Every marriage has its share of losses and pains. Like Jack, we feel loss when we give up a dream for the sake of the relationship. Our spouse feels hurt when we fail to keep our promises. We feel anxious and angry when we argue and nothing gets resolved. We feel stressed out when we are pulled in different directions by conflicting demands.

The greatest obstacles to our growth as a person and as a couple are not the disappointments, the frustrations, the stresses, or even the pains we cause one another. The primary obstacle to our happiness is our denial of them.

Denying the pain

As children of Adam and Eve, we have inherited the tendency to deny what is real by pretending that it is not, by anesthetizing our pains, or by rationalizing to get what we want. We may pretend that no problem exists when a spouse seems distant and withdrawn, or becomes violent. We may tell ourselves that nothing is wrong when a spouse drinks excessively and secretively. We may ignore or avoid unresolved conflicts or recurring arguments. We may dismiss our own feelings of guilt by making excuses or blaming our spouse. Or we may try to escape our own anger, frustration, or depression by keeping busy and burying ourselves in our work, by becoming over-involved in the lives of our children, or by escaping into sports, pornography, or other fantasies.

When we try to ignore our emotional and spiritual pains, we disconnect ourselves from the reality of our life and from each other. When we rationalize or excuse our actions, we are being dishonest with ourselves. We pretend that everything is fine and that we are in control of our life, yet deep inside we know that we are not. We are unhappy and we slowly drift apart.

Although denial may be a helpful coping mechanism to keep us sane in moments of crisis, it is damaging when it becomes a way of life. Denial keeps us from accepting what is real about our life. It keeps us from acknowledging our limitations and sinfulness and from turning to God and one another for help. Denial keeps us from mourning.

Letting go of illusions

Spiritual writers tell us that to overcome denial, we need the courage to accept our spiritual poverty and emptiness. We need to let go of the illusion that we can do everything we set our mind to do, as well as of the expectations that our spouse can meet all our needs or that we can meet all of our spouse's needs.

We have been given many gifts, but we are also imperfect and we sin. When we can be honest with ourselves and accept our own strengths and shortcomings as well as those of our spouse, we can start using our gifts to overcome some of our imperfections.

As a couple we can learn to appreciate each other's gifts and work together to compensate for each other's weaknesses. Then together we can create a life in common that gives us comfort, and we can become an image, although pale, of God's goodness and love.

Helping each other accept what is real

In marriage we can help each other let go of our illusions, embrace our imperfections, and accept the pains and disappointments that life brings. Out of love we can affirm each other's gifts and good qualities. We can lovingly challenge one another's denials and unhealthy ways to escape reality. We can lend an empathetic ear, or give a hug or comforting touch, or offer words of support when one is in pain. We can stand by each other and protect each other in moments of need. We can also encourage each other to seek professional guidance and support if needed. Most of all, we can pray for our spouse and always be sincere with one another. Mother Teresa is quoted to have said: "Let us be very sincere in our dealings with each other, and have the courage to accept each other as we are."[20]

Jack and Grace

Jack and Grace have since started going to church regularly. In addition, they sought professional help to guide them in resolving their many conflicts. He is very talented, and his career is growing and has not suffered because of his lack of geographic mobility. The turning point for him was accepting that life with Grace was going to be different than what he had imagined, and that to find happiness as a couple, both needed to make sacrifices to accommodate each other. On her part, Grace grew to appreciate the sacrifice Jack was making to accommodate her need, and she promised to moderate her expressions of dislike for the extensive business travel required of Jack by his current job.

■ Where do I start?

Knowing "what is" is the first step in resolving a conflict. Ignoring the conflict or avoiding addressing a problem are sources of frustration that drain the good feelings from your relationship. The first step in avoiding denial is trying to understand. When confronted with a conflict with your spouse, rather than withdraw or attack, pause for a moment and seek to understand your spouse's point of view by:

---

20. Mother Teresa of Calcutta, Desmond Tutu, *Love: The Words and Inspiration of Mother Teresa* (Boulder, CO: Blue Mountain Arts, Inc., 2007), p. 51.

- Listening while keeping an open mind.
- If necessary, repeating back what you have heard and what you think it means.
- Having your spouse confirm that your understanding is correct.

This process is demanding. It requires intentionality and self-restraint, especially when emotions are high, but it is worthwhile. Once your spouse knows that you understand, he or she may be willing to listen to your point of view and try to understand. Practice this way of connecting with your spouse in your day-to-day interactions. You will then be ready to use this approach when painful conflicts arise.

"Offer it up"

Disappointments, conflicts and misunderstandings, and the daily sacrifices we make to accommodate each other are our crosses in marriage. Jesus is telling us that to become his disciples, we must let go of our excuses and denials and take up our cross and follow him (Matthew 16:24). Sometimes these crosses may feel unbearable. When this happens, pray with Jesus, "My Father, if it is possible, let this cup pass from me; yet not what I want but what you want" (Matthew 26:39).

Blessed Pope John Paul II encourages us to accept the pains and the discomfort that life brings, without bitterness. They are our crosses through which we join Christ in suffering, for the salvation of all.[21] Blessed Mother Teresa said, "Suffering is nothing by itself, but suffering that is shared with the passion of Christ is a wonderful gift and a

---

21. John Paul II, *Salvifici Doloris* (Vatican City: February 11, 1984), #19.
   "Thus each man, in his suffering, can also become a sharer in the redemptive suffering of Christ."

sign of love."[22]

In his encyclical on hope, Pope Benedict XVI recalls that there was a time when, in the face of suffering, we used to encourage one another to "offer it up." He wonders whether it might be appropriate to revive this counsel again. He writes, "In this way, even the small inconveniences of daily life could acquire meaning and contribute to the economy of good and of human love."[23]

■ Prayer

The Lord is my shepherd, I shall not want.
    He makes me lie down in green pastures;
he leads me beside still waters;
    he restores my soul.
He leads me in right paths
    for his name's sake.

Even though I walk through the darkest valley,
    I fear no evil;
for you are with me;
    your rod and your staff—
    they comfort me.

Surely goodness and mercy shall follow me
    all the days of my life,
and I shall dwell in the house of the Lord
    my whole life long.

■ PSALM 23:1–4, 6

22. Eileen Egan and Kathleen Egan, *Blessed Are You* (New York: MJF Books, 1992), p. 47.

23. Benedict XVI, *Spe Salvi* (Vatican City: November 30, 2007), #40.

■ QUESTIONS FOR **A COUPLE'S PRIVATE REFLECTION**

- Are there conflicts or problems that we (individually or to-gether) avoid facing?

- What are some of them?

- Do you remember your first major disappointment or con-flict in your relationship? What was it about, and when did it happen?

- List two situations that cause discomfort in your relation-ship today.

- Discuss with your spouse changes you may be willing to make to relieve the discomfort in these situations.

- Discuss with your spouse whether you are ready to pray together to ask for God's help and comfort in moments of pain.

■ QUESTIONS FOR **GROUP SHARING**

- In your opinion, what helps spouses most in coping with disappointments or conflicts?

- What are the typical pains that spouses experience in ad-justing to each other as a couple?

- Do you agree that denial is a problem in a marriage?

- What do you think are the impacts on a marriage of exces-sive drinking, use of drugs, pornography, excessive use of video games, and over-involvement in social networks?

- What do you think about the pope's suggestion of "offering up" our pains to join Christ in his work of redemption? How do we teach this concept to our children?

- Can you think of a couple who models the loving attitude of mourning in their marriage?

"Blessed are those who mourn, for they will be comforted."

CHAPTER FOUR

Treat your spouse with respect

Blessed are the meek...

"I'm too tired"

The relationship of many couples can be summed up in the following exchange I witnessed during a marriage counseling session. Margaret and Jim, married fifteen years, sought counseling because they had been arguing about sex. He wanted more. She was always too tired. Sitting in my office, Margaret started the conversation with a litany of chores that defined her life. "In the morning I make everyone's bed. Then I make breakfast, get the kids dressed, and take them to school. I go to my work and later, on my way home, I pick up the kids from daycare. I cook dinner and make sure Chris and Amy do their homework. On weekends I shop for the family, I do the laundry and clean the house. And, by the way, I have a full-time job. I'm exhausted!"

When she paused, the woman was almost breathless, and Jim was looking at the floor and shaking his head as if he had heard this recitation many times. He looked very frustrated. There was a lot of tension in the room. To break the ice, I said, "It makes me tired just listening to you."

Margaret smiled, but her husband ignored my comment. Then, raising his head and looking at Margaret, Jim said angrily, "Don't you complain! I do my part. I work sixty hours a week to keep our business going, and after work I have to entertain clients late in the evenings. My job is what keeps this family going! My load is just as heavy. You do not have to work full time. You're always too busy or too tired when I want to do something with you."

Turning toward me, Margaret said, "Every time we talk about this, we end up going around in circles. We get angrier and angrier until we both blow up, and we walk away without accomplishing anything."

The room was silent for a long time.

Marriage is a team sport

Marriage has been compared to a three-legged race, which requires teammates to coordinate their efforts and to act as one. Jim and Margaret were not acting as members of the same team. If they had been running a three-legged race, they would have experienced many falls and would not have made much progress.

"Blessed are the meek, for they will inherit the earth," proclaimed Jesus (Matthew 5:5). Being meek, as Jesus commands us, does not mean being a wimp and letting others step all over us. Meekness is an attitude that helps us run the marriage race successfully by being sensitive and respectful of each other's wants and needs.

The meekness preached by Jesus in this Beatitude is first of all an attitude of respect toward God. It is acknowledging that God is God and we are his creatures. This attitude of reverence and respect extends also to our relationships with people, especially to the relationship with our spouse. Meekness allows us to work together as an effective team. Margaret and Jim were so wrapped up in their personal pains, anger, and frustrations that they were not able to put aside their emotions long enough to respectfully hear each other's point of view. They were fighting each other and escalating their hostility instead of resolving together their common problem.

How meekness helps

How can meekness help Jim and Margaret? For married couples, meekness means controlling anger and frustration and addressing differences without retaliating. Saint Thomas Aquinas, in his masterpiece the *Summa Theologica*,[24] teaches that meekness is the virtue that moderates passion and anger, and combats our impulse for revenge. Saint Paul, in the letter to the Christians in Ephesus, writes, "Put away from you all bitterness and wrath and anger and wrangling and slander, together with all malice, and be kind to one another, tender-hearted, forgiving one another, as God in Christ has forgiven you" (Ephesians 4:31–32). For couples like Jim and Margaret, meekness means letting their feelings of anger cool down long enough to acknowledge that they have a common problem.

Psychologists know that in marriage, problems are never "my" and "your" problem. They are always common problems. A successful resolution is possible only when each partner considers what he or she contributes to the existence and maintenance of the problem.

Conflicts are unavoidable in any marriage. Some researchers say that as many as sixty-nine percent of conflicts go unresolved, even in

---

24. Thomas Aquinas, *Summa Theologica*. II II.157.1 and 2 (en.wikisource.org/wiki/Summa_Theologiae/Second_Part_of_the_Second_Part/Question_157).

healthy marriages. The presence of conflicts is not a sign of a failing marriage. The difference between successful and unsuccessful couples is how they resolve their conflicts or learn to live with those that cannot be resolved.

Meekness is an attitude that disposes us to hear God's voice and plays a role in facilitating the successful resolution of marital conflicts.

Practicing meekness

John Gottman, author of *The Seven Principles for Making Marriage Work*,[25] gives couples valuable advice, based on his research. He would advise couples like Jim and Margaret to avoid starting their conversation with a criticism or a sarcastic remark that blames the other, such as Jim's comment, "You're always too busy or tired when I want to do something with you." Words such as these make the other spouse feel attacked and become defensive. This approach starts a negative cycle that is likely to escalate hostile emotions rather than lead to a resolution. Instead, he suggests that each spouse, without blaming the other, describe how they see the situation and how it is affecting them.

Jim could have said, "Margaret, I notice that in the evenings you are often exhausted. Can we talk about how I can relieve some of the pressure you feel? I would really like to have more time together with you when we are both relaxed." Gottman calls this approach a "soft start." His advice emphasizes the value of mutual respect in problem resolution.

On the other hand, Gottman would advise Margaret to be aware of timing in approaching Jim with her concerns. Rather than start her litany of complaints when Jim arrives home and is tired, she would do

---

25. Gottman and Silver, p. 159.

better to find a time when he is relaxed, or schedule a time for bringing her concerns to Jim, and say: "Jim, I need to talk to you. I have a problem and I need your help finding a solution…" Timing is important. Bringing up a problem on the way out of the house or before going to bed in the evening may not be conducive to finding a satisfactory outcome for either spouse.

Managing emotions

A second important recommendation from Gottman's research is learning to stop oneself when the emotions are about to get out of hand. Even though a couple may start a conversation calmly, emotions can flare up as the differences are presented. When tension mounts and emotions are about to take over, slow down and even take a break to calm yourself down. Ask for a "time out." Doing so does not mean that you are trying to avoid discussing the subject at hand. It means that you want time to step away to calm yourselves down and to think about the issues rationally, with the promise to return to the discussion after a while.

To me, the effort to bring up a touchy subject gently and respectfully and the willingness to stop oneself before emotions take over the conversation are examples of meekness at work.

■ Where do I start?

Over the next few days, become aware of how you manage your emotions.

- What do you tend to do when you are angry and frustrated? What do you tend to do when you are sad or anxious?

- What impact does your way of managing your emotions have on the relationship?

- If the impact is negative, what can you change?

- Monitor how you bring up a touchy subject to your spouse. Ask yourself: Is my approach inviting my spouse to hear me, or is it perceived as an attack?

- Ask God for help before starting a difficult conversation with your spouse.

- Consider reading Chapter Five of Gottman's *The Seven Principles for Making Marriage Work*.

Making progress

Fortunately, Margaret and Jim were able to draw enough humility and courage from their Christian faith to ask a counselor to help them address their conflict. They agreed to set aside a regular time at home to discuss their recurring conflicts calmly and with mutual respect. They also agreed that in future arguments, either one could ask for a "time out," with a promise to return to the discussion within a reasonable time.

They decided that they did not want to continue fighting the way they had. They took joint ownership for all their many responsibilities. Margaret decided to cut back her hours of work, a move that eased some of her stress. Jim agreed to set aside one evening a week when he would be home for dinner with Margaret and the children, and they would spend time together.

Asking for meekness

Christian spouses find through their faith the graces they need to grow in meekness. Our Catholic tradition links meekness with the gift of "Piety," one of the seven gifts of the Holy Spirit. The gift of piety, explains Blessed John Paul II, "extinguishes in the heart those fires of tension and division which are bitterness, anger and impatience, and nourishes feelings of understanding, tolerance, and pardon."[26]

Ask the Holy Spirit for a renewed outpouring of this gift of piety on you and on your spouse. Remember that Christ is a partner in your relationship and is always ready to help. As the *Catechism* tells us, "Christ dwells with them [the spouses], gives them the strength to take up their crosses and so follow him."[27] With meekness you will experience fewer tumbles in your three-legged race, and most of all, you will make progress on your journey to holiness and grow in your love for each other.

■ Prayer

Take delight in the Lord,
and he will give you the desires of your heart.

Commit your way to the Lord;
trust in him, and he will act.

Be still before the Lord, and wait patiently for him;

Refrain from anger, and forsake wrath.
Do not fret—it leads only to evil.

---

26. John Paul II, *Angelus*, May 28, 1989 (www.vatican.va/liturgy_seasons/pentecost/documents/hf_jp-ii_ang_19890528_en.html).

> "The gift of piety further extinguishes in the heart those fires of tension and division which are bitterness, anger and impatience, and nourishes feelings of understanding, tolerance, and pardon. Such a gift is, therefore, at the root of that new human community which is based on the civilization of love."

27. *Catechism of the Catholic Church*, #1642.

But the meek shall inherit the land,
* and delight themselves in abundant prosperity.*

Our steps are made firm by the Lord,
* when he delights in our way;*
though we stumble, we shall not fall headlong,
* for the Lord holds us by the hand.*

- PSALM 37:4–5, 7–8, 11, 23–24

■ QUESTIONS FOR **A COUPLE'S PRIVATE REFLECTION**

- Am I comfortable with how my spouse brings up a touchy subject? If yes, what do I appreciate about it? If no, what do I dislike about it? What suggestions do I have for my spouse?

- Am I comfortable with the way my spouse controls his or her emotions during a disagreement? If I am uncomfortable, am I willing to share with my spouse what causes me discomfort?

- Are we able to agree to disagree and to compromise without pouting or holding grudges?

- Do either of us have a problem with managing our anger?

- Are we competing with each other in ways that are destructive to the relationship?

■ QUESTIONS FOR **GROUP SHARING**

- Can you identify with the story of Jim and Margaret? Is their situation common?

- What are some of the recurring conflicts that most married couples encounter?

- What are some of the creative solutions couples you know have found to resolve their conflicts with schedules or workloads?

- Are there conflicts in your relationship you have agreed to live with because they require making changes that are too difficult to make?

- What do you think of the technique of taking a "time out" to manage your emotions during a heated conversation? Could it work for you?

- Can you think of a couple who models the loving attitude of meekness in their marriage?

*"Blessed are the meek,
for they will
inherit the earth."*

CHAPTER FIVE

Do what is right

*Blessed are those
who hunger and thirst
for righteousness…*

On the road

Mary, a young sales executive, is traveling for the first time with her manager, Jack, a middle-aged vice president of marketing in a fast-growing company. Jack and Mary have been on the road together for the past five days. They crisscrossed the country from Atlanta to Chicago, Boston, Los Angeles, and then San Francisco, where they will spend the weekend while waiting to meet a customer on Monday.

They spent yesterday and today sightseeing together and now, Sunday evening, they are sitting in the hotel restaurant for a drink and dinner. Jack talks about his family and his last vacation in Colorado with his children. Mary, who is single, talks about her dreams. She talks about Mark, her boyfriend, and what they like to do together. She talks about missing him.

During their dinner and relaxed conversation, Jack notices how attractive Mary is and how comfortable he feels in her company. He enjoys being with her in a casual setting and likes to hear her talk. He has been feeling this way all weekend while they were sightseeing. The awareness of these feelings stands in contrast with the lingering anger toward his wife of twenty-five years, from the argument they had just before he left home a week ago.

After dinner Mary and Jack walk to the elevator while reviewing one more time the schedule of the next day's activities. When the elevator stops at Jack's floor, he turns to Mary and says politely, "Good night!"

Mary grabs his hand and says with her delightful smile, "Wait! Come to my room for a drink. I have enjoyed very much this weekend with you!"

Jack is taken aback, not expecting this invitation. He hesitates for a moment. The idea is enticing but he knows this is not right. He responds, "Mary, thank you very much for the invitation. It is getting late and I promised my wife I would call her." Then, as he steps out of the elevator, he says, "Good night! I'll see you tomorrow."

Doing what is right

Jesus proclaimed, "Blessed are those who hunger and thirst for righteousness, for they will be filled" (Matthew 5:6). Jesus is calling us to be aware of our soul's longing for God and of our inner desire to do what is right in God's eyes. Pope Benedict writes about this Beatitude, "God demands…that we become inwardly attentive to his quiet exhortation, which is present in us and which tears us away from what is merely habitual and puts us on the road to truth."[28] That is what Jack did. Although Mary's invitation might have been innocent, Jack listened to the voice inside that said: "This is not right." He did not want to put himself in a situation that could compromise, first, his faithfulness to his wife and, second, his role as Mary's manager.

Jesus calls all husbands and wives to do what is right by keeping the promises they made on their wedding day. In our vows we promised to be true in good times and in bad, in sickness and in health. Those sacred promises are what hold us together as a couple. They give stability to our life in common. Because of them we can count on each other. It is on promises kept that we build our trust, and it is through growth in trust that we open ourselves to an intimate relationship with our beloved.

Thornton Wilder wrote in his play *The Skin of Our Teeth*:

> I didn't marry you because you were perfect…I married you because you gave me a promise. That promise made up for your faults. And the promise I gave you made up for mine. Two imperfect people got married and it was the promise that made the marriage.

Broken promises

Unfortunately, broken promises have become a part of our cultural landscape. Friendships at work or online have become the latest threat to marriage. Today we are experiencing a crisis of fidelity, writes Shirley P. Glass, PhD, in her book *NOT "Just Friends."* This new infidelity, she explains, is between people who call themselves "just friends."

---

28. Joseph Ratzinger, *Jesus of Nazareth* (New York: Doubleday, 2007), p. 92.

Glass continues, "Today's workplace has become the new danger zone of romantic attraction."[29] More time is spent with coworkers than with one's spouse. Men and women in the workplace become friends and form deep connections. At times, before they realize it, they cross the line between friendship and romantic infatuation. Shirley Glass reports that affairs happen even in good marriages. She adds that most affairs today have less to do with love and more to do with sliding across boundaries. This is exactly what Jack sensed could happen in his relationship with Mary because of his feelings and her invitation.

Sliding boundaries and technology

Sliding boundaries can be facilitated today by modern technologies like email, texting, and social media sites and chat-rooms. While such technical advances can bring people together, they can also drive wedges between spouses. Consider how often, when we are together, we let incoming text messages, emails, or phone calls interrupt our conversations. New technologies are helpful but, if not managed, can act as distractions from the spousal relationship. In their homes husbands and wives may find themselves sitting next to each other while deeply immersed in interactions with others through social media sites.

A short time ago a marriage and family therapist wrote to me, "I have counseled a number of couples recently where one partner's time on Facebook has been very problematic. In a couple of cases, one spouse has met or reconnected with an old friend and the relationship violated the marital boundary." The Internet is a door that offers boundless opportunities for connecting intimately with out-

---

29. Shirley Glass, PhD, *NOT "Just Friends"* (New York: Free Press, 2003), pp. 1-2.

siders. Unfortunately, its use can become harmful when we allow old flames, friends met in chat rooms, or pornography to intrude into our relationship.

Pornography is a special threat to the marriage because of the attitude it promotes. The Church teaches us that sexual intercourse is not just a biological act. It is a sign, writes John Paul II, of a total self-giving of one person to another.[30] This personal self-giving is absent in pornography. The *Catechism* teaches us that pornography perverts the conjugal act.[31]

Checking our boundaries

Glass encourages spouses to check their boundaries by asking themselves such questions as:

> Do I confide more to my friends than to my spouse about how my day went?
>
> Do I discuss negative feelings about my marriage with my friends and not with my spouse?
>
> Would I feel uncomfortable if my spouse heard my conversations with my friends?[32]

Affirmative answers are red flags of danger for your marriage. They should alert you to sliding boundaries. They should warn you that what you are trying to satisfy outside of your marriage is something you need from your spouse.

---

30. John Paul II, *Familiaris Consortio*, #11.

31. *Catechism of the Catholic Church*, #2354.

32. Shirley Glass, PhD, *NOT "Just Friends,"* p. 16.

Computer etiquette

To encourage spouses to live their commitment and to protect their boundaries, Chris Gersten has produced a Couples Computer Protocol.[33] Chris is a former principal deputy assistant secretary, Administration for Children and Families, Department of Health and Human Services. This protocol encourages spouses to have complete transparency in computer use. To learn more visit the website of the Fatherhood and Marriage Leadership Institute (www.famli.us). There you will find helpful suggestions, such as:

- Share your password with your spouse, or have just a single account with a common username and password.

- Let your spouse know that he or she is welcome to look through your emails, or social network accounts.

- Promise not to visit open-ended chat-rooms and personals sites, or pornographic sites.

- Promise not to engage in IM conversations of a private and/ or provocative nature.

- If contacted by former boyfriends/girlfriends on social networking sites, let your spouse know, and ask for their input/ recommendations on how to respond.

A good suggestion for families is to keep the family computer in an open space. Marriage experts recommend that one should not cruise the Internet when tired, lonely, or upset with one's spouse. They suggest that when we go online, we should have a specific destination in mind. If we are easily tempted to check out pornographic sites, ask the

33. Chris Gersten, *Internet Rules for Couples*, December 8, 2009 (FAMLI website: www.famli.us/index.php?option=com_content&view=article&id=77%3Acou ple-computer-protocol&catid=43%3Ainformation-and-resources&Itemid=1).

help of our spouse or a trusted friend to keep us accountable. They can block our access to such sites, or install web-tracking software. Jesus said in the Sermon on the Mount, "If your right hand causes you to sin, cut it off and throw it away; it is better for you to lose one of your members than for your whole body to go into hell" (Matthew 5:30).

Self-mastery

"Blessed are those who hunger and thirst for righteousness, for they will be filled" (Matthew 5:6). To achieve the promise of this Beatitude, husbands and wives need to develop their ability to control their senses, their passions, and the human impulse to seek immediate gratification. This self-mastery gives us the freedom to choose what is right. Our Catholic tradition teaches us that we grow in this self-mastery through the practice of the moral virtues. Among these are prudence and temperance. Through these virtues, we form habits that affect the way we act. Through prudence we avoid situations that can lead us astray, and through temperance we enjoy the pleasures of life within the bounds of God's design for us.

The virtue of temperance is often associated with chastity. Yes, chastity is a virtue that applies to married couples. The United States Catholic bishops in their pastoral letter *Marriage: Love and Life in the Divine Plan*, call all married couples to love with conjugal chastity. They explain, "The practice of marital chastity ensures that both husband and wife will strive to live as a gift of self, one to the other, generously."[34] The practice of chastity does not mean the suppression of our natural desire for affection and sexual intimacy. We live chastely when we recognize these needs and integrate them in our relation-

---

34. *Marriage: Love and Life in the Divine Plan* (Washington, DC: USCCB, 2009), p. 48.

ship in a way that through our body we become a gift to our spouse. Sexual intercourse is an act of self-giving, an expression of love and not merely a pleasure-seeking act.

■ Where do I start?

- Consider whether any of your relationships with friends and coworkers can lead to sliding boundaries.

- Intentionally and graciously accommodate your spouse's wishes even if it requires some sacrifice on your part.

- Ask yourself: Do I see myself as a gift to my spouse, and do I act like one in sexual intercourse?

- Learn the meaning of chastity in marriage. Read from *Marriage: Love and Life in the Divine Plan* the section titled "Growth in the Virtues" (pages 46-51).[35]

The need for God's grace

Progress in self-mastery and growth in righteousness are possible with the help of the Holy Spirit. For Christian spouses the temptations to deviate from doing what is right is not less real than for anyone else, and the growth in self-mastery is not less difficult.

When we are resolved to do what is right and we seek God's help, the power of his grace gives us the strength to succeed. Christ, who is present in our marriage, makes up for the weakness of our will. All we need to do is to listen to him. He encourages us as he did for Saint Paul when he was facing his own human weaknesses: "My grace is sufficient for you" (2 Corinthians 12:9).

---

35. Find it at: www.usccb.org/laity/.

Make it a habit to listen to the voice that comes from your conscience. Grow in self-mastery. Always treat your spouse with respect. Your healthy habits will keep you on the right path. That is what Jack did in a split-second decision when Mary invited him to her room for a drink. He acted prudently and avoided a situation that could have threatened his marital commitment and his career.

■ Prayer

Hear my prayer, O Lord;
    give ear to my supplications in your faithfulness;
    answer me in your righteousness.
Do not enter into judgment with your servant,
    for no one living is righteous before you.

Let me hear of your steadfast love in the morning,
    for in you I put my trust.

Teach me to do your will,
    for you are my God.
Let your good spirit lead me
    on a level path.

I believe that I shall see the goodness of the Lord
    in the land of the living.
Wait for the Lord;
    be strong, and let your heart take courage;
    wait for the Lord!

■ PSALM 143:1–2, 8, 10; 27:13–14

■ QUESTIONS FOR **A COUPLE'S PRIVATE REFLECTION**

- What is the understanding that you and your spouse have about your use of the Internet? Are you comfortable with it?

- If you do not have a clear understanding with your spouse on how each of you should use the Internet, take a few moments to discuss how each of you wants to be responsible and accountable in using this tool.

- What would your spouse say about his or her ability to count on you to do what you say you will do in your day-to-day interactions? In other words, how do you keep the daily promises you make?

- What do you do to keep your friendships with persons of the opposite sex from interfering with your marriage?

■ QUESTIONS FOR **GROUP SHARING**

- What is your understanding of chastity in marriage?

- Create a list of tips for spouses on how to relate with friends and coworkers of the opposite sex at work or in social settings. List what is acceptable and what is not.

- What are your thoughts about using the Internet and social media safely and prudently? What are your suggestions for married couples?

- What is the value of self-mastery in helping you grow in love with your spouse?

- Have you found yourself in situations similar to what Jack experienced in the story of this chapter?

- Can you think of a couple who models the loving attitude of hunger and thirst for righteousness in their marriage?

"Blessed are those who hunger and thirst for righteousness, for they will be filled."

CHAPTER SIX

Learn compassion

Blessed are the merciful…

You deserve a break!

"I am sorry that it took me so long," said my wife, Teri, as she walked in the kitchen carrying grocery bags. "I stopped at the store for a few groceries and ran into Eileen, a friend from church. Her daughter just got married. She told me that she worked so hard to prepare for the wedding that at the end she was exhausted. After the wedding, when all the celebrations were over and they had dropped off their last houseguests at the airport, she and her husband, Jim, went home with the intention of cleaning the house. Jim surprised her when he said, 'You have an hour to pack. You worked hard preparing for this wedding. You deserve a break! The laundry and the house will still be here when we return.'" Teri continued, as she was putting the groceries away, "Eileen said that this was the best thing Jim could have done for her. They went to Gatlinburg, in the Smoky Mountains, and she slept for a whole day to catch up. Wasn't that nice of Jim?"

Yes, what Jim did for Eileen was very nice. He showed mercy toward his wife. She needed rest, and he understood. He also knew that she would not recuperate if she stayed at home. Jim felt compassion and provided the relief she needed.

Living the works of mercy

"Blessed are the merciful, for they will receive mercy" (Matthew 5:7). In this Beatitude, Jesus calls married couples to live the "works of mercy" first in their spousal relationship and then in their community. The *Catechism* teaches us that the works of mercy are charitable actions through which we meet the physical and spiritual needs of others.[36] The corporal and spiritual works of mercy give us the opportunity to show God's mercy to those near us who are in need of consolation, comfort, advice, support, forgiveness, and prayer.

Jim put into practice the counsel of this Beatitude; he provided comfort and support to his wife. In marriage, being attentive to our spouse's needs and responding with our help is an act of mercy and compassion.

His needs, her needs

Dr. Willard Harley, Jr. writes in his book, *His Needs, Her Needs: Building an Affair-Proof Marriage,*[37] that every person has emotional needs. We depend on others to meet some of these needs. Young lovers are attracted to each other because each sees in the other something they desire, and they marry committing to meet certain intimate needs for one another. In their wedding vows, couples promise to be there for

---

36. *Catechism of the Catholic Church*, #2447.

37. Willard F. Harley, Jr., *His Needs, Her Needs: Building an Affair-Proof Marriage* (Grand Rapids, MI: Fleming H. Revel, 2008), pp. 18-19.

each other in good times and in bad, in sickness and in health, no matter what happens.

To find happiness in marriage, Dr. Harley exhorts his readers, "Become aware of each other's emotional needs and learn to meet them."[38] Such needs, according to Dr. Harley, are so important that when they are left unmet, spouses are tempted to go outside the marriage to satisfy them. He identifies some of the most basic needs spouses want to have met in marriage. Among these are: affection, sexual fulfillment, companionship, admiration, honesty, and openness. Helping each other meet our individual emotional needs is an act of love that expresses mercy.

Compassion

Doctors Patricia Love and Steve Stosny write in their book, *How To Improve Your Marriage Without Talking About It,*[39] that compassion makes us sensitive to the individuality and vulnerability of our spouse. Compassion makes us aware of our spouse's needs, and when we act on it, we show mercy.

Benedict XVI, in his book *Jesus of Nazareth,*[40] ties the message of this Beatitude to Jesus' parable of the Good Samaritan in Luke 10:29–37. He explains that the Samaritan's heart was open and receptive. He allowed himself to be touched by the need that he saw in the person who had been robbed and beaten. "He had compassion," writes the pope. Benedict explains that this parable is relevant to every human being because each one of us is in need of healing and everyone is called to respond like the Good Samaritan.

---

38. Harley, p. 17.

39. Patricia Love and Steven Stosny, *How to Improve Your Marriage Without Talking About It* (New York: Broadway Books, 2007), Ch. 11.

40. Ratzinger, *Jesus of Nazareth*, p.197.

A wife can be a Good Samaritan when, in her compassion, she notices her husband's stress and discomfort and in mercy respects his space with silence, instead of peppering him with questions. She offers support with sympathetic eye contact, or a physical gesture, or a touch that says, "I understand. I am here."

A husband has the opportunity to be a Good Samaritan when he notices that his wife is anxious, or feels insecure. He shows mercy toward her by being present to her pain and listening to her feelings instead of suggesting what she should do to fix her problem. "The bottom line is: Be there with your partner's feelings. Don't ignore them, try to 'fix it,' or try to talk about it or drag him or her out of it,"[41] write Love and Stosny. What counts is not doing for my spouse what feels good for me, but doing what helps my spouse feel better and heal. This is an act of self-giving love. This is mercy.

Learning to connect

Dr. Gary Chapman, in his landmark book *The Five Love Languages*, recognizes the importance of being sensitive to each other's needs. He then goes a step further. To respond to each other's needs, he explains, spouses need to connect effectively. He writes, "We must be willing to learn our spouse's primary love language if we are to be effective communicators of love."[42]

In his experience as a marriage therapist, Chapman identified five primary love languages spouses use to connect with each other. They are: words of affirmation (compliments, words of appreciations, encouragement, kind words of support), quality time (undivided at-

---

41. Love and Stosny, p. 159.

42. Gary Chapman, *The Five Love Languages: How to Express Heartfelt Commitment to Your Mate* (Chicago: Northfield Publishing, 1995), p. 15.

tention, taking a walk together, sharing one's day over a meal, doing something together that is fun), receiving gifts, acts of service (cooking, washing dishes, taking out the garbage, painting the bedroom, washing the car), and physical touch. He reports that all too often spouses speak different love languages and, in spite of all good intentions, their needs for intimacy are often unmet.

■ Where do I start?

We are called to become as merciful as Jesus. This encourages us to develop an awareness of our spouse's needs and to reach out to help in a way that our spouse appreciates. Here is how you can start today.

- Identify one of your spouse's emotional needs, such as affection, admiration, honesty, sexual fulfillment, or companionship.
- Try to identify your spouse's love language. Observe how your spouse responds to your expressions of affection and love, and identify what she or he appreciates the most.
- In the next few days be attentive to your spouse's needs and, moved by compassion, reach out to help; offer mercy.
- Read Dr. Chapman's book *The Five Love Languages.*

Listen to God's whisper

In the Sermon on the Mount, Jesus invites us to holiness. In this Beatitude he encourages us to be merciful toward one another. Spouses can express mercy by showing compassion for their partner's needs and reaching out to help, as the Good Samaritan did.

The attitude of mercifulness is not something we can achieve on our own. We are the wounded children of Adam and Eve. We tend to be selfish and look out for our own needs first. We need God's grace to make up for our deficiencies. To help us, Christ gave us his Spirit, who guides us with the gift of "Counsel," one of his seven gifts.

Open your heart to hear God's counsel, and be inspired to be merciful through the prayer of Saint Francis. Let this prayer lead you to pay attention to your spouse's needs: to notice the stress on your spouse's face, to listen to the pain or frustration in his or her voice, to be present in moments of pain and give comfort, and to respond to your spouse's requests with kindness. Let this prayer make you sensitive to the needs not only of your spouse but also of people in your community who need your compassion and your help.

As Blessed Mother Teresa said, "Be the living expression of God's kindness: kindness in your face, kindness in your eyes, kindness in your smile."[43]

■ Prayer

> *Lord,*
> *make me an instrument of your peace.*
> *Where there is hatred, let me sow love;*
> *Where there is injury, pardon;*
> *Where there is doubt, faith;*
> *Where there is despair, hope;*
> *Where there is darkness, light;*
> *Where there is sadness, joy.*
>
> *O Divine Master,*
> *grant that I may not so much seek to be consoled as to console;*

---

43. *Mother Teresa Words* ©Mother Teresa Center, exclusive licensee throughout the world of the Missionaries of Charity for the works of Mother Teresa. Used with permission.

To be understood as to understand;
To be loved as to love.

For it is in giving that we receive;
It is in pardoning that we are pardoned;
And it is in dying that we are born to eternal life.

- PRAYER OF SAINT FRANCIS

■ QUESTIONS FOR **A COUPLE'S PRIVATE REFLECTION**

- Recall a time when your spouse recognized a need of yours and reached out to help. Share with your spouse how you felt on that occasion.

- List two of your spouse's emotional needs, such as affection, sexual fulfillment, companionship, admiration, honesty, etc. Share these with your spouse, and ask him/her to validate or correct your perceptions.

- What do you think is your spouse's primary love language, as defined by Chapman? Share your perception with your spouse, and ask for validation.

- Ask your spouse to share with you his or her needs that are least met.

■ QUESTIONS FOR **GROUP SHARING**

- How would you define "compassion"? Give examples of how you have experienced compassion in your life.

- From your own experiences, do you agree that compassion is a necessary quality in marriage? Why or why not?

- Can you give examples of how your spouse helps you meet some of your needs?

- The *Catechism* lists the following actions as spiritual works of mercy: instructing, advising, counseling, comforting, forgiving, and bearing wrongs patiently. Discuss how these apply to marriage.

- The *Catechism* lists the following actions as corporal works of mercy: feeding the hungry, sheltering the homeless, clothing the naked, visiting the sick and imprisoned, and burying the dead. Discuss how these apply to marriage.

- Can you think of a couple you know who models the loving attitude of mercifulness in their marriage?

"Blessed are the merciful, for they will receive mercy."

CHAPTER SEVEN

Express gratitude

Blessed are the pure in heart…

Bathed in God's love

During workshops for married couples, I often ask the participants, "How do you feel God's presence in your relationship?" This question leaves many puzzled. So I help them by saying, "What feelings or actions in your relationship make you think of God?" Many respond by saying, "I think of God when I am scared." "When I am in pain." Some say, "When I am happy." "When I see my children playing, or when they are sick and I feel helpless to relieve their pain."

I remember in particular the answer of a young couple I met several years ago. Lynn and Matt had been married one year. Seeing them together, there was no doubt that they were in love. They were very physical and demonstrative in their affection. When I asked them to share what feelings and actions in their relationship made them think of God, Matt looked at Lynn as if to seek reassurance, then hesitantly, and with a nervous smile, said, "What makes me think of God is how

61

I feel when I am close to Lynn, like right now." He was sitting close to her and holding her hand. "Lynn's physical presence, her touch, her beauty and her interest in me make me feel complete. When I feel like this, I thank God for the gift that she is to me. It's like God made Lynn just for me."

Lynn, who had been looking at Matt with an admiring gaze, chimed in, "I feel the same way. When Matt touches me, and caresses me, or helps me, I feel cared for and loved. Those feelings are so good that they make me thank God for him. This is especially true when we make love. My whole self feels bathed in love, and I feel a deep sense of gratitude." She stopped and, with a bashful smile, said, "Well…this is getting too personal…but you know what I mean."

Matt and Lynn could see God through their interactions because in faith they understood that each was God's gift to the other, and they treated each other as such. "Blessed are the pure in heart, for they will see God" (Matthew 5:8).

Have you ever thought that the goodness you were cherishing in your spouse was a taste of God's goodness? Benedict XVI writes, "The organ for seeing God is the heart."[44]

The dance of lovers

The United States Catholic bishops remind us of what God intended when he created marriage. They write in their pastoral letter on marriage, "Adam and Eve were literally created for each other."[45] God made man and woman to be a gift for each other.

With his death on the cross, Jesus taught us that the essence of true love is self-giving. The honest gift of oneself to one's spouse is a re-

---

44. Ratzinger, *Jesus of Nazareth*, p. 92.

45. *Marriage: Love and Life in the Divine Plan*, p. 10.

minder of the goodness of God. Benedict XVI says, "Every form of gift is…a sign of the presence of God."[46]

The adventure of falling in love is driven by the desire to know the gift that is our beloved. The dance of lovers consists of movements of self-giving and self-disclosure. With each step of this dance, we share more of the person that we are. Each act of self-revelation increases the intimacy and strengthens the relationship. This journey we call love is exhilarating to the extent that the sharing is done with a pure heart. Love is a gift of oneself that is founded on honesty and transparency. When it is such, love becomes the window through which we can see God. Love without honesty and transparency is not love. Yet, we find ourselves often hiding our goodness from one another because of our lack of openness with each other.

Gratitude

Openness and transparency are essential for love, but the true joy of loving comes from gratitude. It comes from our ability to see the precious gift that our spouse is and to appreciate and cherish it. Just as Adam exclaimed in joy, "This at last!" (Genesis 2:23) when he first saw Eve, every husband and wife marveled in the same way when they first saw their mate. Such joyful marvel is an expression of awe and gratitude to God.

That sense of thankfulness for the gift of each other extends to the everyday life of the couple. "In joyful gratitude for his wife, a husband gives himself completely to his wife; and in gratitude for her husband,

---

46. Benedict XVI, *Address to Envoys of Nepal, Zambia, Andorra, Seychelles and Mali*, December 16, 2010. ZE10121803 - 2010-12-18 (Permalink: www.zenit.org/article-31280?l=english).

"Every form of gift is, in a word, a sign of the presence of God, because it leads to the fundamental discovery that, at the origin, everything is given."

a wife gives herself completely to her husband,"[47] write the United States bishops in their pastoral on marriage. This spousal gratitude is expressed most joyfully in the self-giving of sexual intercourse. From the mutual love of husband and wife, this sense of gratitude overflows to the family, and from the family to the community. It is our gratitude to God for the gift of life.

Living God's plan

The invitation of this Beatitude to live our life with purity of heart is also a call to live our marriage according to God's plan and design. Spouses entering a sacramental marriage choose to live their life with a purpose: to love and to serve God in everything they do. On their wedding day, Catholic spouses embrace each other as mates, and together they embrace Christ as a partner in their marriage, seeking his help to follow God's plan for them. One of the touch points between humanity and divinity in a marriage is the intimate act of collaborating with God in the creation of new life.

Matt and Lynn felt God's presence in their life, including their lovemaking, because through their faith they recognized the gift that God had given them in sexual intercourse. Through sexual intercourse, spouses give themselves totally to each other, a giving that unites them and bonds them as a couple. At the same time, a man and woman place themselves and their fertility at God's service in the creation of new life. Sexual intercourse is a gift that has the power to bind the spouses together and to create new life.

It is an act of total self-giving to each other and of self-giving to God in the service of life, if such is his will. This is why, as Catholics, we believe that sexual intercourse should always be open to the creation of new life.

---

47. *Marriage: Love and Life in the Divine Plan*, p. 50.

Natural family planning

To stay in tune with God's design for the creation of life, many couples, Catholic and non-Catholic, have found a way to harmonize their life and lovemaking with their natural cycles of fertility as designed by God. They use various methods known under the umbrella name of "natural family planning." These methods help couples track their fertility for the purpose of achieving pregnancy or postponing it. These methods of natural family planning are totally safe, healthy, and reliable in regulating births. The use of these methods encourages husband and wife to stay attuned to God's will and to work as a team to exercise their shared responsibility for their fertility. The benefit of this approach is an increased communication between husband and wife and a greater appreciation of each other's unique roles in God's design for life.

Benedict XVI explains, "The Church affirms natural regulation of conception, which is not just a method, but also a way of life. Because it presupposes that couples take time for each other."[48]

The challenge to couples choosing to live with openness to life by using natural family planning methods is the required self-discipline.[49] This self-discipline can become especially trying and can demand considerable sacrifice at difficult moments in a couple's life. It is in these moments that Catholic couples, because of their faith, feel the power of God's grace. Pope John Paul II reminds us that we are not alone. He said in his homily during his visit to the Mount of the Beatitudes in 2000, "Jesus does not stand by and leave you alone to face the challenge. He is always with you to transform your weakness into strength.

---

48. Benedict XVI, *Light of the World: A Conversation with Peter Seewald* (San Francisco: Ignatius Press, 2010), p. 147.

49. You can find information about natural family planning programs in your area by going to the website of the United States Conference of Catholic Bishops (www.usccb.org/prolife/issues/nfp/index.shtml).

Trust him when he says: 'My grace is enough for you, for my power is made perfect in weakness' (2 Corinthians 12:9)!"

The gift of understanding

In this Beatitude Jesus calls us to be "pure in heart." He invites us to be honest with ourselves and with our spouses. He exhorts us to live our married life according to God's original intent and to rejoice in the many gifts God gives us in marriage. Our joy and love are sacraments, visible and tangible signs of God's goodness and love. On our journey to holiness, we depend on God's help to grow in purity of heart.

At baptism you received the gift of "Understanding," one of the seven gifts of the Holy Spirit. To grow in purity of heart, ask the Holy Spirit to help you understand and appreciate the gift that God has given you in marriage.[50]

■ Where do I start?

Lynn and Matt were able to "see" God in each other's presence because they recognized and appreciated the goodness of God's gift in each other's personality and sexuality. Consider the suggestions below, and do as many as you can.

- Become aware of moments in your relationship when you "see" God's goodness and love in your spouse.
- List three qualities of your spouse that you consider a gift.
- Thank God for each of them.

---

50. A tool you can use to grow in your understanding is the pastoral letter on marriage written by the United States Catholic bishops: *Marriage: Love and Life in the Divine Plan.*

- Today find a way to let your spouse know how much you appreciate these qualities.

- Read *Marriage: Love and Life in the Divine Plan*.

Be open to God's grace

Living your marriage according to God's plan is not easy and requires sacrifice. Ask Christ to help you. The *Catechism of the Catholic Church* teaches us that God never refuses the graces that spouses need: "To heal the wounds of sin, man and woman need the help of the grace that God in his infinite mercy never refuses them. Without his help man and woman cannot achieve the union of their lives for which God created them."[51]

The fruits of a pure and grateful heart are the joys of marital intimacy. These joys are a taste of heaven, daily moments when we "see" God, and an invitation to remember that God is the source of all gifts. Yes, God made your spouse just for you. Only purity of heart will help you "see" not only how special is the gift, but also how good is the Giver.

■ Prayer

> *O Lord, you have searched me and known me.*
> *You know when I sit down and when I rise up;*
> *   you discern my thoughts from far away.*
>
> *Even before a word is on my tongue,*
> *   O Lord, you know it completely.*

---

51. *Catechism of the Catholic Church*, #1608.

For it was you who formed my inward parts;
  you knit me together in my mother's womb.
I praise you, for I am fearfully and wonderfully made.
  Wonderful are your works;
that I know very well.
  My frame was not hidden from you,
when I was being made in secret,
  intricately woven in the depths of the earth.
Your eyes beheld my unformed substance.
In your book were written
  all the days that were formed for me,
  when none of them as yet existed.

■ PSALM 139:1–2, 4, 13–16

■ QUESTIONS FOR **A COUPLE'S PRIVATE REFLECTION**

- Recall special moments in your relationship that made you aware of God's presence.

- Tell your spouse how he or she is a gift from God to you.

- Share with your spouse your understanding of what God's design for marriage is.

- What is your experience with natural family planning?

■ QUESTIONS FOR **GROUP SHARING**

- What do you think the Church means when it says that marriage is a vocation?

- What is your understanding of how the Church looks at sex within marriage?

- What do you know about natural family planning? Is training available in your diocese for couples who wish to learn it?

- What role do honesty and gratefulness play in your ability to grow in intimacy?

- Can you think of a couple you know who models purity of heart in their marriage?

*"Blessed are the pure
in heart,
for they will see God."*

CHAPTER EIGHT

Forgive

Blessed are the peacemakers…

Not the whole story

A friend shared the story of his marriage over lunch. He said, "When I got married, I believed I had hit the jackpot. There I was, a poor boy from Tennessee marrying a well-educated and successful executive from a New York firm. She was making three times my salary, driving a company car, a brand new BMW, and talking about a promising career with her firm. As we dated, we dreamed of a big home, nice cars, and expensive vacations to exotic places."

"Lucky you, Jim!" I said to my friend.

Shaking his head, he replied, "That is not the whole story. Six months after the wedding, Mary was pregnant. We were both excited. Then, after our first-born came along, Mary made a sudden career change. She decided she wanted to stay home and be a full-time mom to our son. That was a shock to me. This meant that I had a big mortgage, a wife and a child to support, all on my very meager salary. I was scared, and became very angry. During the first twelve months of our son's life, Mary and I argued a lot about all sorts of things. There was a war going on between us. Underlying all the painful skirmishes was the deep resentment I felt. I felt cheated and wanted to retaliate! This was the point in our relationship where I could have let my bitterness turn me away from Mary and conclude 'I want out of this situation. This is not what I had bargained for. It certainly isn't what we dreamed our life would be.'"

I asked, "What happened? You are still together, aren't you? How did you make it?"

Problems are part of life

I don't know how many couples have had a similar situation. However, I am certain that all couples sooner or later encounter relational problems that hurt their marriage. Some of these may be easy to resolve and to forget, but others are serious and may even threaten the relationship, such as a spouse being irresponsible with the use of the family money, having an affair, suffering from a serious addiction, and many others. All of these bring with them much pain, especially for the spouse who feels wronged.

"Blessed are the peacemakers, for they will be called children of God," preached Jesus (Matthew 5:9). How does anyone bring peace to a relationship full of turmoil? How did my friend and his wife find peace in their situation?

He explained. "What kept us together was our faith. Not knowing what to do, I turned to God for help and asked him to guide me and to give me the strength to discuss this subject with Mary without letting my anger get in the way. First, however, I needed to let go of the thought that I had been cheated, and of the 'poor me' attitude. I had to forgive Mary and myself for the injuries we caused each other in our fighting. At the same time, I was acutely aware and pained by the fact that we needed to find a resolution to our financially untenable situation. It took me a while to muster the courage to bring up the subject in a calm manner to Mary, and I prayed for help. I finally did talk to her. Mary listened and then said, 'To me, money is just money and we don't need many of the things we have.' She believed that our son needed the love and the presence of one of us at home more than we needed the material things we had. I could not disagree. I felt the same way, but I did not like the conclusion that these thoughts were leading us to. I wanted for her to work and earn an income. After many heart-to-heart conversations on this subject, we decided to downsize our home and to live on a budget we both could agree on and that would fit our limited income."

I think that my friend had the right attitude and the right answer to this predicament. He wanted a resolution to their financial problem, but most of all, he wanted peace in their home. The key to the success of this couple was their ability to forgive and to move on with life.

Finding true peace

True peace in a marriage is not possible without forgiveness, according to both family therapists and Blessed John Paul II. The pope proclaimed in his World Day of Peace message on January 1, 2002, "No peace without justice, no justice without forgiveness." The Italian psychologist Roberto Assagioli writes, "Without forgiveness life is governed by an endless cycle of resentment and retaliation."[52] Lack of forgiveness creates an environment of tension that festers with acts of aggression. In such an environment, one can hear sarcastic remarks, such as "Yes, dear!" that mean "No! Leave me alone." One

---

52. University of Kentucky—College of Agriculture, Honesty, Forgiveness, and Love, October 31, 2011 (www.ca.uky.edu/hes/fcs/possibilities/Media_Articles/22-Honesty_Forgiveness_and_Love.htm).

can also witness verbal and physical abuse, lies, silent treatment, and other dysfunctional interactions that pull spouses apart and hurt the marriage.

In addition, lack of forgiveness negatively affects the mental and physical health of the person who carries the burden of being the victim. Mark Twain is quoted to have said, "Anger is an acid that can do more harm to the vessel in which it is stored than to anything on which it is poured." Similarly, Melva Johnson, a relationship counselor, writes on her website, "Those who condemn their spouses to hell because of their unwillingness to forgive, sentence themselves there as well."[53]

Forgiveness requires courage

To forgive, we need spiritual strength and courage. Mahatma Gandhi said, "The weak can never forgive. Forgiveness is the attribute of the strong." Jesus gave us a clear example of great courage when, on the cross, he prayed for those who were killing him, "Father, forgive them; for they do not know what they are doing" (Luke 23:34).

My friend Jim and his wife, Mary, needed courage to let go of the anger and to put behind them all the hurts they had inflicted on each other. Each of them had created a wall for self-protection during their months of skirmishes, grudges, and unresolved conflicts. That wall was kept up by pent-up resentment toward each other, and it was destroying their marriage. Through their faith Jim and Mary found the courage to gradually tear down the wall. In the privacy of their hearts, they acknowledged their own contributions to the deterioration of their relationship and turned to God for forgiveness. Benedict XVI

---

53. Mining for Gold Marriage, March 27, 2011 (mfgmarriage.com/forgiveness-in-marriage).

writes, "Only the man who is reconciled with God…and with himself can establish peace around him and throughout the world."[54] It was only after accepting personal responsibility for their own shortcomings and reconciling with God that Jim and Mary could reach out to each other and reconnect.

For Catholic spouses this process of reconciliation can be facilitated by the sacrament of penance (that is, reconciliation) and the graces that accompany it. The *Catechism of the Catholic Church* teaches us that, "without being strictly necessary, confession of everyday faults (venial sins) is nevertheless strongly recommended by the Church."[55] Regular confession helps form our conscience, and through it we let ourselves be healed by Christ.

Confessing our faults

In the Sermon on the Mount, Jesus said to the crowd gathered before him, "When you are offering your gift at the altar, if you remember that your brother or sister has something against you, leave your gift there before the altar and go; first be reconciled to your brother or sister, and then come and offer your gift" (Matthew 5:23–24). Being reconciled with God is an important step in healing, but it needs to be followed by reconciliation with one's spouse. Such happens through one's admission of wrongdoing. James writes to the early Christian communities, "Confess your sins to one another, and pray for one another, so that you may be healed" (James 5:16).

The reason many couples argue endlessly and hold long grudges is because neither spouse wants to admit to the other that he or she has made a mistake or done something wrong. Many of us find it dif-

---

54. Ratzinger, *Jesus of Nazareth*, p. 85.

55. *Catechism of the Catholic Church*, #1458.

ficult to say "I was wrong. I made a mistake, please forgive me." Chuck Lynch writes that most of us have made it a habit to simply say "I'm sorry," expecting forgiveness.[56] Unfortunately, this often does not satisfy the person offended because "I'm sorry" lacks a direct admission of fault. Saying "I'm sorry" can mean I am sorry for the way you feel, or I am sorry that you misunderstood my intentions, but it does not say "I was wrong, please forgive me."

What is often missing in our interactions is the confession of our wrongdoings. Such admission of fault builds a bridge to forgiveness and reconciliation. I am not saying that we should not use the words "I'm sorry." We need to express our sorrow, but it must be accompanied by our verbal admission of fault, a request for forgiveness, and a promise not to repeat it.

■ Where do we start?

We begin the process of forgiving by recognizing our own imperfections, admitting our faults, and asking God for his mercy and forgiveness. To grow in your relationship with God and with your spouse, take a moment to examine yourself. Place yourself mentally in God's presence, and ask yourself:

- What actions or words of mine have offended my spouse recently?

- Single out one that may still be causing pain today.

- Acknowledge your shortcoming, and express your sorrow to God for your wrongdoing.

56. Chuck Lynch, *Don't Say You're Sorry*, *Kyria*, May 12, 2011 (www.kyria.com/site/utilities/print.html?id=59983).

- Imagine how you would ask forgiveness of your spouse, admitting what you did wrong. Be specific, such as "I was wrong when I…I am sorry. Please forgive me."

- Ask God for the courage and the inspiration to say the right words that heal.

- Reach out to your spouse, admit your faults, and ask forgiveness.

- Consider availing yourself of the healing power of the sacrament of penance (reconciliation).

Finding peace with God's grace

My friend Jim and his wife, Mary, succeeded in finding peace because, when disappointed and overwhelmed by their situation, they humbly turned to God and to each other for help. Graced with the gift of "Wisdom" that they received from the Holy Spirit at baptism and confirmation, they admitted to each other their shortcomings and their individual contributions to their strife, and they forgave each other. Then they negotiated an agreeable solution to their problem. They adjusted their lifestyle to the income they were making. Their healing was not sudden or a onetime event. It was gradual. Forgiveness does not heal all the wounds immediately. Forgiveness gives the space for the wounds to heal over time.

◼ Prayer

> *To you, O Lord, I lift up my soul.*
> *O my God, in you I trust;*
> > *do not let me be put to shame;*
> > *do not let my enemies exult over me.*
>
> *Make me to know your ways, O Lord;*
> > *teach me your paths.*
> *Lead me in your truth, and teach me,*
> > *for you are the God of my salvation;*
> > *for you I wait all day long.*
>
> *Turn to me and be gracious to me,*
> > *for I am lonely and afflicted.*
> *Relieve the troubles of my heart,*
> > *and bring me out of my distress.*
> *Consider my affliction and my trouble,*
> > *and forgive all my sins.*

▪ PSALM 25:1–2, 4–5, 16–18

◼ QUESTIONS FOR **A COUPLE'S PRIVATE REFLECTION**

- Recall a time when you felt hurt because of your spouse's actions or words. How difficult was it for you to forgive and to reconcile?

- When you experience disappointments and hurts caused by decisions made by your spouse, how do you respond?

- How do you restore peace in your relationship after a conflict? Which of you is most likely to take the first step to reconcile?

- Can you recall a time when you were upset with your spouse and you prayed for him or her?

■ QUESTIONS FOR **GROUP SHARING**

- Discuss the importance of forgiveness in a marriage.

- Can you think of betrayals that are unforgivable? Is anything unforgivable?

- Imagine how a person who cannot forgive his or her spouse might feel? Describe that feeling to the members of your group.

- Put yourself in Jim and Mary's situation. What would you have done?

- Discuss how the sacrament of reconciliation is a tool for growth in marriage.

- Can you think of a couple you know who models peacemaking in their marriage?

"Blessed are the peacemakers, for they will be called children of God."

CHAPTER NINE

Stand up for what you believe

*Blessed are those
who are persecuted
for righteousness' sake…*

Refusing evil

The theme of mourning and suffering addressed by Jesus in the second Beatitude is also found in the last Beatitude, in which Jesus says that those who are persecuted for the sake of righteousness are blessed. We may be tempted to dismiss the relevance of this Beatitude because today the word "persecution" does not appear often in our newspapers or television broadcasts. However, Benedict XVI, in his book *Jesus of Nazareth*, reminds us of what persecution means for us today. He writes that the type of suffering Jesus is talking about in his last

Beatitude is the pain we experience when we refuse to conform with evil. It is the pressure and the discomfort we are made to feel when we resist going along with certain trends and behaviors that are accepted in society because "everyone does it." He writes, "The world cannot tolerate this kind of resistance; it demands conformity."[57]

A new culture

Some time ago on a business trip to Stockholm, Sweden, I invited several colleagues to dinner. These were professional men and women in their late twenties and early thirties. During the meal, the young lady that was sitting next to me started complaining about her "partner." She said, "My partner is never home in the evening. We are at the point that we hardly see each other. We are more like roommates." Her comments caught the attention of the whole table, and a discussion ensued about relationships. Realizing that most people sitting at the table were not married but were living with another person—a partner—I asked, "Why don't you get married?" The entire table laughed. I was told that people there didn't get married right away. They live together and then, if they are right for each other, they get married. The group proceeded to tout the benefits of premarital cohabitation. It was obvious to me that these intelligent individuals were well indoctrinated in the social norms and expectations of their culture.

Upon my return home I searched the Internet for "Cohabitation in Sweden." I found several studies indicating that in this Nordic

---

57. Ratzinger, *Jesus of Nazareth*, pp. 87-88.

"The mourning of which the Lord speaks is nonconformity with evil; it is a way of resisting models of behavior that the individual is pressured to accept because "everyone does it." The world cannot tolerate this kind of resistance; it demands conformity."

country premarital cohabitation is the norm, so much so that over fifty percent of children born in Sweden are born outside of marriage. I also found that eighty percent of women who cohabit and then marry end up divorcing. So much for using cohabitation as a way to see if "we are right for each other." This is sad because this social practice is placing children, the next generation, at risk. It creates a family environment that is unstable because the adult parental figures come and go from their life. Most psychologists agree that a stable home environment is very important to a child's healthy development.

Unfortunately, this same mentality has taken root in the United States. Some authors are writing that premarital cohabitation seems to be replacing dating. Today more than half of all first marriages are preceded by living together, compared to virtually none fifty years ago. This is regrettable because not only is cohabitation morally wrong, but a substantial body of evidence indicates that those who live together before marriage are more likely to break up after marriage.

Recently I taught a Sociology class on Marriage and the Family at a local university. To my surprise I found that ninety-nine percent of the students in my class believed that cohabitation is good, something to be recommended as a way to prepare for marriage. I was reminded of my conversation with coworkers in Sweden. At the end of the course, I asked my students to comment on what they had learned that was important to them. I was pleased to find that several listed, as valuable knowledge, the statistics they had learned in the textbook about cohabitation and its pitfalls.

The influence of "secular individualism"

Cohabitation is but one of the many symptoms of a cultural shift taking place in today's society. The authors of "The State of Our Unions,"[58] a report issued by the National Marriage Project, attribute this cultural shift to the growing influence of "Secular Individualism." Secular individualism is a mindset that is spreading across all modern cultures. This secular view of life abandons the guidance of religious faith and replaces it with the pursuit of personal self-fulfillment as the guiding principle. This view is leading our society to distort the meaning of marriage; accept cohabitation, divorce, and abortion; condone promiscuity; downplay commitment; and belittle the value of a life guided by religious faith. As Catholics we are caught in a culture war. We are challenged daily to accept popular values and behaviors that are contrary to the principle of self-giving love and sacrifice proclaimed in the gospel. All around us a fierce battle is going on to capture our minds and our hearts. Benedict XVI describes what is happening as "a poisoning of thought."[59]

The culture war

The relevance of the last Beatitude for us today has been underscored both by Blessed John Paul II and Benedict XVI in their descriptions of the present social culture. John Paul II in particular told us of a raging battle between the culture of life and the culture of death. Benedict XVI defines this struggle as "a clash of two spiritual worlds, the world of faith and the world of secularism."[60] Marriage and family life are at

---

58. The National Marriage Project, *The State of Our Unions 2007* (Rutgers, NJ: July 2007).

59. Seewald, p. 48.

60. Seewald, p. 57.

the center of this battle, and each one of us is called to choose sides. The family, in particular, is the battleground in this war because, as John Paul II said repeatedly, "As the family goes, so goes the nation and so goes the world in which we live." The United States bishops urge us in their pastoral letter on marriage: "We call upon them [Catholic faithful] to stand against all attacks on marriage and to stand up for the meaning, dignity, and sanctity of marriage and the family."[61]

The weapons in this culture war are very subtle. They are disguised in images, words, and sounds that are all around us. We see and hear them in song lyrics, video games, films, commercial advertisements, television programs, Internet sites, and other means of social communication. Today many messages enter our homes encouraging instant self-gratification, exalting individualism, and promoting materialism. They pressure our children and us to conform. Their intense noise can drown out the sound of God's voice deep inside our hearts.

Parents need to become alert to the messages of self-indulgence that are seeping into our family's culture and are weakening our Christian values. Pay attention to what your family sees and hears through television shows, movies, video games, songs, and the Internet.

We need to also protect ourselves and our families from today's prevailing thought that proclaims that there are no limits to what we can do, there are no rules except the rules we make, and there are no truths that are absolute. We live in a secular society that pretends it has no need for God.

Unfortunately, managing today's information overload entering our homes with its anti-religious messages is a new experience for many parents. We learned from our parents how to protect our children from physical dangers, but we have no example from them on how to protect our family from today's erosion of our Christian values coming from modern communication and social media.

---

61. *Marriage: Love and Life in the Divine Plan*, p. 4.

◼ Where do I start?

So, what can you do? The first thing we can all do is to become aware of who and what is influencing our thinking and our actions, as well as who and what is influencing our children.

- Become aware of the TV shows you are watching. Pay attention to their messages.

- Ask yourself: "Do I agree with the lifestyles portrayed through the media?"

- Become informed on what we believe as Catholics. Use the *Catechism of the Catholic Church* as a resource. Read articles in your diocesan newspaper to stay informed.

- Read passages from the Bible and pray together as a family.

Ultimately, we need to remember that what is most important in teaching our children right from wrong is our personal example. Pope John Paul II reminded us that the Christian family passes on the faith when parents teach their children to pray and when they pray together with them.[62] As a Christian couple, through the gift of faith, you have the benefit of God's grace and of the guidance of the Catholic Church's teachings.

God's grace

In baptism and in confirmation, you received the gift of "Knowledge" from the Holy Spirit, the ability to know the truth. Ask the Holy Spirit for the wisdom to discern what is harmful to your family and what is not. Read God's word in the Bible. Seek the guidance of the Church. The *Catechism of the Catholic Church* is an excellent compendium of

---

62. John Paul II, *Familiaris Consortio*, #60.

what we believe and of the Christian principles that guide our decisions. Prayer is always an important tool for staying connected with God and for listening to his voice. Ask the Holy Spirit for the courage to take a stand and to resist the pressures of your social environment that are contrary to the gospel values. Your family needs your guidance, and you need the help of God's grace.

The apostle Paul exhorts us: "Do not be conformed to this world, but be transformed by the renewing of your minds, so that you may discern what is the will of God—what is good and acceptable and perfect" (Romans 12:2).

■ Prayer

In you, O Lord, I seek refuge;
*   do not let me ever be put to shame;*
*   in your righteousness deliver me.*
Incline your ear to me;
*   rescue me speedily.*
Be a rock of refuge for me,
*   a strong fortress to save me.*

You are indeed my rock and my fortress;
*   for your name's sake lead me and guide me.*
Into your hand I commit my spirit;
*   you have redeemed me, O Lord, faithful God.*

■ PSALM 31:1–4, 5

■ QUESTIONS FOR **A COUPLE'S PRIVATE REFLECTION**

- Remember a situation in which you felt your Christian values were challenged.

- What TV shows are most popular in our home?

- What values do the shows we watch portray?

- How can we help each other protect our children from the secular values that surround us?

- How can we help each other teach our children our Christian values?

- What are our family prayer traditions?

- What are the ways in which you pray together as a couple and as a family?

■ QUESTIONS FOR **GROUP SHARING**

- What are the values and views about marriage and family most prominently displayed on TV programs and movies?

- How do these differ from the Christian views of marriage and family?

- How do you control your children's access to television and social media?

- How can we inoculate ourselves, our children, and our grandchildren from the influence of the culture of self-indulgence that surrounds us?

- What do we do to listen to the guidance of the Church in living our Christian life?

- How do you stand up for what you believe?

- Can you think of a couple you know who models Jesus' call to stand up for what we believe?

*"Blessed are those
who are persecuted for
righteousness' sake,
for theirs is the
kingdom of heaven."*

Ordinary holiness

The parish church was packed with tearful eyes. Jim's body was in an open casket in the center of the sanctuary, and a procession of mournful men and women filed slowly to bid their farewell.

Why so many people? Who was this person?

Jim was an active parishioner and a family man. He was a devoted husband to Norma and a good father to their children. The same friends and people of the parish who came to say good-bye to Jim had gathered two months before to witness Jim and Norma's renewal of their wedding vows on the occasion of their fiftieth wedding anniversary.

Fighting the odds of advanced cancer, Jim promised Norma, "I will be here for our anniversary. Let's have a big celebration with our friends and family."

So they did. That evening Jim and Norma were surrounded by their children, grandchildren, and friends to celebrate their life together, all the while knowing that Jim's end was near. Dressed in a tuxedo, Jim was beaming and mustered all of his strength to get up and dance with

Norma, his daughters, his eight-year-old granddaughter, and his sisters. From time to time he would return to his seat to take some deep breaths from his portable oxygen tank.

Several years ago, Teri, my wife, and I had the privilege of joining Jim and Norma on a team that prepared young couples for marriage. We still remember their sharing with the young couples how they learned to love each other and the struggles they had to understand and to accept each other's unique personalities. They talked about the adjustments they had to make to accommodate each other's preferences, and about Norma's decision to become Catholic. During their sharing, they narrated their battles and the most tender moments of their life, and they both had to pause several times to dry their tears. Their commitment prevailed, and their life together was a witness to all of us of what Christian married love is about.

Living holiness

Jim and Norma are one of the many ordinary couples in parishes all over the country aspiring to holiness. These couples don't talk about holiness, but they live it. Their actions show it. They are not perfect, but they try each day to be the best they can be for one another.

During their fifty years of marriage, Jim and Norma helped each other along on the path of life. Their path was not straight nor was it easy. They, like all of us, found the Christian married life challenging. There may even have been times in their marriage when their path was so unclear that they felt doubt or thought they were lost. It was then that they trusted their faith and followed the guidance of the Church and the promptings of God's voice speaking to them in their heart.

"Holiness does not consist in never having erred or sinned," says Benedict XVI. "Holiness increases the capacity for conversion, for repentance, for willingness to start again and, especially, for reconciliation and forgiveness."[63]

In this book, we have reflected on the Beatitudes as the sign posts pointing toward holiness on the path of life. John Paul II said to the youth gathered in Toronto at the Seventeenth World Youth Day,

> "The eight Beatitudes are the road signs that show the way. It is an uphill path, but he walked it before us. He said one day: 'He who follows me will not walk in darkness (John 8:12).'"[64]

In the Beatitudes, we learn the loving attitudes that help us grow in holiness: poverty in spirit, mourning, meekness, purity in heart, peacefulness, mercifulness, and suffering for the sake of Christ. These attitudes open our heart to hear God's voice and to follow its promptings. The more we master these attitudes, the happier we are in our marriage because holiness is the source of our joy.

A few weeks after Jim's funeral, Teri and I attended a friend's birthday party. As we were parking, we saw Norma, who was driving a brand new car. She greeted us and exclaimed, "See what Jimmy bought me?" She explained that three days before Jim died, he instructed one of his lifelong friends and his brother to make sure that she got a new car. "This is what I want her to have," he said to them.

Norma continued, "He was concerned that I would have problems with the older car and that he would not be around to help me. Oh, how I miss him," she sighed. "He was trying to take care of me to the very end, and I know that he is still watching over me."

---

63. Benedict XVI, *General Audience*, January 31, 2007 (www.vatican.va/holy_father/benedict_xvi/audiences/2007/documents/hf_ben-xvi_aud_20070131_en.html).

64. John Paul II, Papal Welcoming Ceremony, Seventeenth World Youth Day, Toronto, July 25, 2002.

The love of Jim and Norma is the mature love that Benedict XVI describes in his encyclical on love: "Love now becomes concern and care for the other. No longer is it self-seeking…; instead it seeks the good of the beloved: it becomes renunciation and it is ready, and even willing, for sacrifice."[65]

God's love song

Deep within your heart,
if you listen,
you hear God's voice.[66]

He sings to you his eternal love song:
the song through which he created the universe,
the stars and the moon, the flowers,
    the birds and all creatures.

It is the song through which God
formed you in your mother's womb
and called you out of it
to love him and to serve him.

God's song is the music that attracted you to your spouse;
the rhythm that moves you to dance together;

---

65. Benedict XVI, *Deus Caritas Est*, #6.

66. Pope Benedict XVI, *Greeting to the Youth of London after Mass in Westminster Cathedral*, September 18, 2010.

> "Deep within your heart, he is calling you to spend time with him in prayer…We need to make space for silence, because it is in silence that we find God, and in silence that we discover our true self. And in discovering our true self, we discover the particular vocation which God has given us for the building up of his Church and the redemption of our world."

the melody that leads you to grow in love with each other;
and the voice that calls you to serve God
   as a married couple.

God invites you to sing with him his love song,
and to dance to its rhythm.
Listen to it.
Learn it,
and
with Christ's help
dance, and sing along with him.

That is holiness!

APPENDIX

Use the chapters of this book as springboards for reflection and conversation with your spouse when using the accompanying video program "Beatitudes: A Couple's Path to Greater Joy."

Below is the order in which the content of the chapters of this book is addressed in the video program.

VIDEO 1	Your marriage is your call to holiness
	Read Introduction
	Chapter 1: "Blessed are they…"
	Chapter 2: "Stay turned toward God and each other"
VIDEO 2	Your marriage is a dance
	Read Chapter 3: "Accept what is"
	Chapter 9: "Stand up for what you believe"
VIDEO 3	Your marriage is a three-legged race
	Read Chapter 4: "Treat your spouse with respect"
	Chapter 8: "Forgive"
VIDEO 4	Your marriage is your treasure
	Read Chapter 5: "Do what is right"
VIDEO 5	Your marriage is your home
	Read Chapter 6: "Learn compassion"
VIDEO 6	Your marriage is a celebration of life
	Read Chapter 7: "Express gratitude"
	Conclusion

JOHN BOSIO

John Bosio is a husband and father, a seasoned family life educator, a former marriage and family therapist, and a retired global corporate manager. He and his wife, Teri, volunteer their expertise in religious education and family life to their diocese and parish, and conduct workshops and retreats for married couples around the country. John writes a monthly column on marriage for the *Tennessee Register*, the newspaper of the Diocese of Nashville.

John and Teri have been married for thirty-nine years. They have two daughters, a son-in-law, and a grandson. John brings to this book a well-rounded experience as an educator trained in theology, a counselor trained in marriage and family therapy, and a corporate manager experienced in global human resource management.

John was born in Italy and moved to the United States to pursue undergraduate and graduate studies. A theology graduate of The Catholic University of America and of Saint Paul's College in Washington, DC (MA in theology, 1970), John also earned a master's degree in counseling in 1977, from the University of Missouri in Kansas City, and completed his training in marriage and family therapy with Family Institute Associates in Kansas City.

John was a member of the American Association for Marriage and Family Therapy (AAMFT). For four years, John and Teri served on the staff of the Archdiocese of Kansas City, Kansas, as a member of the Family Life Office, involved in designing a family life pastoral plan and leading programs in marriage preparation, marriage enrichment, and support groups for divorced Catholics. For thirteen years, he served two parishes in Kansas with a practice in marriage and family therapy. He has held the positions of training and development manager, international HR manager for large enterprises, and most recently the position of global HR manager for Caterpillar Financial Services Corporation, where he supported executives and employees located in over forty countries. John has written many articles on religious education and family life for a variety of publications. John is the author of *Happy Together: The Catholic Blueprint for a Loving Marriage*.